THANK GOD I DIED

Praise for *Thank God I Died*

"This book offers the reader a powerful insight on how a child copes with the extensive emotional and physical trauma they face in a home that embodies abuse. The author shares her journey of the obliteration of her innocence, emotional paralysis, survival and ultimate triumph. Her story is a call to action and recognition of the difference everyone can make if we just act. She also brings inspirational optimism to survivors. It is a powerful read."

—Ginger S., Denver Victim Advocate

"This well written and intriguing book will certainly raise awareness regarding the tragedy of child abuse. It contains a message of hope and redemption amidst a most difficult account of childhood suffering. As illustrated in this story, there is always hope, future and forgiveness available to survivors of childhood abuse."

—Susie Martinez, MA, LPC

"Finally, an author who "gets it"! The unexplained shame and anxiety. The lapses in time where you thought you must have been daydreaming. But why the tears? From a survivor's perspective this book is spot on. I was a little tentative to read it at first. I didn't want more memories coming out. But in the end, I now know that even if they did come, I could handle it. I know I am not alone. I am not the only one. We can accomplish this together! All of us!"

—A survivor

"Jane's gritty and real reflections serve as a reminder that behind every report, every piece of paper that crosses my desk, a real person is affected... Her story shines a bright light, as a beacon of hope and possibility towards the path of resiliency for others to follow. Jane demonstrates that victimization doesn't have to define you but rather presents a narrative that allows you to define yourself."

—**Scott M. Snow, Director, Crisis Services Division, Denver Police Department**

THANK GOD I DIED

A MEMOIR

JANE A. CHANDLER

Thank God I Died: A Memoir
Published by Aspen Trail Press
Lakewood, CO

The names of people in this book have been changed. Some identifying traits have also been changed to prevent character recognition.

Copyright ©2017 Jane A. Chandler. All rights reserved.

No part of this book may be reproduced in any form or by any mechanical means, including information storage and retrieval systems without permission in writing from the publisher/author, except by a reviewer who may quote passages in a review.

All images, logos, quotes, and trademarks included in this book are subject to use according to trademark and copyright laws of the United States of America.

Library of Congress Control Number: 2017949779

ISBN: 978-0-9991589-2-0

FAMILY / Abuse / Child Abuse

QUANTITY PURCHASES: Schools, companies, professional groups, clubs, and other organizations may qualify for special terms when ordering quantities of this title. For information, email AspenTrailPress@StoptheCycleTogether.com

All rights reserved by Jane A. Chandler and Aspen Trail Press.
This book is printed in the United States of America.

To my husband and best friend Rob, for your faith and continuous support on this journey together.

Acknowledgments

Thank you to my editor Bobby Haas. First my editor and now my friend, I couldn't have written this book without your calm and gentle coaching, humor and support.

A PERFECT STORM

I Am Born

The sweltering, muggy heat shoved away the sweet springtime like a menacing bully in the summer of 1960. Air conditioning was a luxury no one in our neighborhood could afford. The intense evening heat drew families outside, under covered porches and large shade trees. As the sun retreated and the relentless heat abated, a transition began. An occasional, gentle breeze provided cool relief to families as they quietly relinquished another summer day. The stars gingerly illuminated the black sky, and the crickets began their sultry evening chorus, seducing all into the hush of the still night air.

That summer's stifling heat foreshadowed years of abuse and a harsh reality as I made my entrance into the world in early July. Raised in the suburbs outside of a large city in the Midwest, my childhood journey appeared to the outside world to be pretty conventional. I was raised with four other siblings in a Catholic home. I would have never picked the family into which I was born, but since I had no choice in the matter, my life of survival began.

My wooden crib hugged the small-screened window for any whisper of cool air. Raggedy Ann came alive on the simple, hand-sewn curtains as she shimmied to the rhythm of the oscillating fan. My cries echoed my arrival to the neighborhood as the final addition to the established family of two brothers, two sisters, and two parents. The handsome white picket fence and neatly trimmed bushes surrounding our little bungalow suggested an idyllic, peaceful home. The neatly positioned pickets created the allusion of solid wood, staked firmly into the earth, yet they merely pretended to envelope our yard with protection. Appearances can be deceiving. Night shadows reflected the home's cracking shingles under the strain of seasons, and those white pickets were actually gray and dingy from disrepair. I guess you would have to look closely to notice, and no one ever did, or no one ever dared look inside. I certainly wish someone had.

My father was typical of World War II veterans. He came home to the suburbs of a large town in the Midwest to marry his sweetheart. They found inexpensive housing in the north area of town, and soon a proliferation of children exploded out onto the streets of our small neighborhood. Predominately Catholic, the neighborhood families produced babies almost faster than they could name them. No wives worked, and most homes had only one car, and even that was a true luxury. Crying babies, mothers scolding children, kids playing in the streets and back yards, and unabashed family squabbles echoed through the neighborhood. My innocent existence within the gentle, safe silence in utero exploded at birth with a raucous cacophony of commotion that brought the outside alive.

A Dark Fairy Tale

However, on the inside, our small house resembled a dark, scary citadel, which was filled with lies and forbidden secrets. Lowered drawbridges and dense foliage presented an unassuming portico by day. But at night, when the drawbridge was raised, grotesque creatures lunged at your ankles for the sick pleasure of spawning terror in the most vulnerable. Behind the buttress, a heartless king and cruel, controlling queen dictated the rules and edicts. No one would recognize they were the same couple who smiled sweetly to neighbors and attended church in the village. The first-born prince despised the laws imposed upon him by the monarchy. Anger oozed from his entire being. Two twin maidens kept their eyes down and spoke only when spoken to. The youngest lad was a blond, blue-eyed boy; my entrance disrupted this chain of power. My soft, blonde curls and gentle, green eyes wanting for fun deflected none of the anger and cruelty that settled in the heavy air of the castle. We all had our roles, and we learned to play them well. We all wanted to survive. It was such a perfectly manicured, neat home, with smiles and politeness and decorum: Who would have known? We played our roles so well that no one could see it was a well-rehearsed performance.

My Brothers, My Sisters

Anthony, the prince, ten years older than me and eight years older than Mike, was, per family tales, not impressed with our intrusion into his life. Anthony and Mike shared a room but not a kinship. Little blond, blue-eyed Mike frequently fled Anthony's verbal and physical assault. His many pleas to our mother eventually lost any real impact, and they became annoying background din. Mom and Dad teased Mike and told him he was too sensitive. This only emboldened Anthony with the thrill of the victimizer's power, the attainment of which was, in fact, Anthony's primary life goal. Extremely intelligent, Anthony used his wits and lies to terrorize and charm. The tyrant flipped like a coin into a pleasant and completely credible martyr, feigning a deep hurt from unjust accusations. Anthony's interminable power and control, plus his incredible intelligence and turnkey charisma, confounded even the smartest adults. Unbridled power became his identity. As his siblings, we saw right through him. We avoided Anthony's cruelty and despised his charming charade. Survival required constant hypervigilance, an exhausting but necessary skill Mike and my sisters mastered. I too would learn this skill.

Anthony's intelligence meant he excelled academically far beyond his classmates, but his academic achievements were overshadowed by his cruelty and obvious lack of empathy. His fist left marks on your skin for weeks, and his hateful words left marks on your heart for decades. The next oldest were twin sisters, eight years my senior. Jenny and Debbie were passive, even meek at times. They learned how to cajole my mother by doing extra household chores to keep themselves in her good graces. I was jealous of their good-girl personas as I watched how those personas often helped them avoid Mom's anger. My brother Mike was just two years older than me. So much chaos and unimaginable atrocities occurred within that home; the neatly trimmed bushes and well-kept yard could only whisper the secrets that lay within. As a child, I kept those secrets hidden in darkness. But one day when I was an adult, an emotional storm knocked me to the ground, and the clouds of silence passed. Those hidden secrets would finally be exposed by the light of truth.

No matter what wickedness lurked within our family's home, I suppose I maintained what appeared to be a normal childhood because, as I look back now, I never recall anyone giving the slightest indication of sensing something may have been very wrong behind those walls. Were my girlfriends curious about my panic related to going straight home after school? Were they ever confused with my intermittent days of melancholy that I tried so hard to conceal? Did extended family members or teachers see hints of abuse when they witnessed my extreme anxiety and tears? Why did no one ever suspect that maybe I wasn't a nervous child at all but actually a hostage in a family of horrors? Did no one see the signs? It probably wouldn't have mattered if I had been questioned. I would have denied anything was wrong. I would not have been able to tell them what was really happening because I couldn't. I had no memory of it—no recall—only the remnants of depression, anxiety, and sadness that plagued me for decades.

Regardless of what took place in our family, life trudged on. School and friends and large extended family gatherings filled my days. The most amazing part was that I somehow was able to compartmentalize. I played. I went to school. I had friends. Mike and I often played Wiffle ball, Kick the Can, and dodgeball with kids on our street until we heard the factory whistle blow in the distance and we all scrambled home for the evening.

Into the World

If I had been able to explain the reasons for the terror that so often gripped me, maybe someone would have paid more attention. But back then who would have been labeled crazy—my parents, the perpetrators, or me—the victim? With no memories to provide context, I learned to act. It was a good act, but it was an exhausting charade. I was never labeled an imposter, so I must have performed very well. In fact, I was so good at repressing memories and squelching emotions that I even convinced myself, at least temporarily. While sleep should have been my solace, the dread of waking up some mornings more exhausted than when I went to bed was a mystery that confused me and created even more anxiety. I was trapped, running aimlessly with no understanding of where I was headed. To survive, I had to keep moving, so I just kept going.

Despite all I endured, I somehow maintained good grades through all twelve years of schooling. I pushed myself to achieve, and eventually my grades allowed me the opportunity to attend a local university. Four years flew by. I graduated, passed my state boards, and started my career as a registered nurse. Nursing was my vocation, and it provided the financial independence for me to leave my home behind, but the acting was not yet over. Just like so many of my friends, I met my husband and married soon after graduation. Shortly after the wedding, I was proudly standing in the warm, cozy kitchen of our new small home. Everything was falling into a natural pattern except for the fights. My husband and I couldn't figure out how to stop a vicious cycle of misunderstanding and arguing. The fights were scaring me. I didn't want to create chaos, so I had to learn to do the opposite of what I grew up with. The only model I had was my parents, and they definitely didn't know how to communicate in healthy ways. But they sure knew how to fight!

My Parents

My mother's childhood began in a tiny, run-down, one-bedroom flat with an angry, sometimes-violent father. Mom was the last of four girls raised in poverty during the Depression. Her parents had emigrated from Northern Europe. She was unusually close to her mother. Grandma was very plump and rosy cheeked, with a quiet laugh. If she wasn't saying a Rosary in her sitting room, she was baking or cooking in her tiny kitchen, which had small cherry tiles bordering the wall across from the sink. Her sweet apple strudel was my very favorite, but her cookies, pies, and candy were decadent delights that melted in your mouth after a fried chicken dinner or a hot bowl of cabbage soup. Every day without fail, Mom would call Grandma at least once, if not more often. Mom was thrilled when a house became available for sale directly across the street from my grandparents. Dad seemed equally excited. We moved just as I entered grade school. This changed our lives. With Grandma as a backup, Mom accepted a job offer against my father's wishes. He was enraged. The day Mom announced her new job, I knew my parents were up arguing until four in the morning because I heard them. I was supposed to be sleeping, but in the middle of the night I was jolted out of a deep sleep and frightened to hear such a commotion. My father was yelling, "No wife of mine is going to work. Your job is at home with the kids." I fell back to sleep and never spoke of that night until years later. I came home from college for Christmas break. I was sharing with my mom what type of nursing I planned to pursue when I graduated. That led to a conversation about Mom's first job. Mom confirmed that I had heard my father's words correctly and explained she thought Dad felt embarrassed and worried that others would think less of him as a man because he could not provide for his family. It obviously didn't matter what my dad said; my mom went to work, we had more chores to do, my older sisters became my babysitters, and we got a second car. I don't know if their relationship was damaged after her stubborn refusal to obey my dad or if his ego suffered from her defiance. Mom and I never spoke of it again. Some things didn't change. We still ate dinners together, we all still kept going to church as a family on Sundays, and Mom still called Grandma every single evening without fail.

While there appeared to be no overt animosity, Mom was not nearly as close to her father as she was to her mother. I imagine it was because he was a man and they just had less in common. While working as a carpenter, Grandpa was quiet and unassuming, so it was surprising to me when Mom spoke of him being drunk and violent when she and her sisters were little. Mom occasionally described some of her dad's physical violence; my grandmother was often the target of his drunken rage. In fear, the four little sisters hid huddled together under their bed. Peering out from under their hideaway, they listened and watched as the horror unfolded, helpless to intervene. Occasionally, her father's brother lived with the family when he was unemployed. Mom despised him.

My father's childhood began in a large brick home with a grieving, broken family. Dad grew up in the same large neighborhood as Mom, but they did not know each other in childhood. Also a child of the Depression, my father grew up in a family that was prominent and affluent because his father was a doctor. They lived in a stately two-story brick home directly adjacent to the Catholic Church rectory. On the other side of their home was an Irish family with eight boys, all older than my father. Unfortunately, Dad never experienced a life of privilege because he was the last of nine children and his father died unexpectedly when Dad was only six months old. Six siblings had already married and moved out of the family home, creating their own lives. The two sisters who were left at home were mere teenagers when they became primary caregivers to my father because their mom had a debilitating neuromuscular disease. Years later at family gatherings, Dad and his eight siblings spoke affectionately of their mother as a kind woman with a quick laugh and generous heart who was initially confined to a wheelchair and then eventually to bed. I remember his two older sisters reflected on how difficult life had been. Their mother's declining health required complete care, so Dad was often left to care for himself when he was only seven years old. Finally succumbing to her illness, Dad's mother died when he was eleven. After the death of their mom, the two older sisters went to work. No longer receiving financial help from their older siblings, they raised Dad as best they could while working to provide food and basic necessities for the three of them. Dad had no male authority figures and minimal supervision.

My parents met right after Dad graduated from high school, and after only a few dates he was drafted during World War II. While he was stationed in Hawaii for a year, their daily letters were the only interaction they had before they married a month after his discharge. Neither of my parents had good role models. Who knows what my mother's father really did when he was drunk or why she so vehemently hated her uncle? What damage did they inflict? I can only imagine what may have happened to my dad as a young boy, with little supervision, raised next to a houseful of priests on one side and, as my aunt described them, eight out-of-control Irish brothers on the other. My father was a prime target for abuse. He was neglected physically and emotionally due to dreadful family circumstances. Since his mom was slowly dying and his sisters were mere teens themselves, neglect was not intentional but inevitable.

Therapists and researchers agree that most adults who sexually abuse children were in fact victims of sexual and physical abuse themselves and were often neglected. These victims then respond to that abuse, neglect, betrayal, and horrible sense of powerlessness by trying to control others, including the exercise of sexual control over children. Some who sexually abuse children still have sexual relationships with age-appropriate partners as they continue abusing kids (Hopper, 2017). We tend to think of pedophiles as secretive, dirty old men who live alone and lure young children into their lair. But that stereotype prevents us from seeing child sexual abusers in our neighborhood or even in our own family. So it's not surprising that my father could have fathered five children and also molested his children or other families' children. The very real probability that my father was abused provides insight into how the cycle of abuse continues and why I was so fortunate to have stopped it.

As a newlywed standing in my own warm, cozy kitchen, all I knew was that I couldn't continue the fighting; I couldn't repeat the brawls of my parents. But how do you change your own behavior when you have never experienced anything else? I never had the opportunity to learn what healthy was. As a child, all I knew was that there were frequent, scary fights and I often felt tremendous anxiety during their battles and even when they weren't fighting. Screaming, crying, slammed doors and hours or even days of my mother terrifyingly ignoring me was the soundtrack to my childhood. The perfectly manicured lawn, white picket fence, and five kids who attended Catholic schools concealed a plethora of secrets. As kids we would ask one another, "Which Mom do you think will come home from work today? Nice Mom or Mad Mom?" One evening Mom would get home from work in a good mood, finish making dinner, ask us about our day, and life was OK. Other days, an immediate cloud of palpable annoyance and irritability followed her through the door. That mad Mom, who was ready to explode without warning, trapped us in a constant shroud of fear. One wrong word, one forgotten chore, one real or imagined slight, and mad Mom's tirade would erupt. My father would take his first opportunity to retreat to the TV room and quickly fall asleep, leaving us kids to fend for ourselves.

Saturday found everyone busy doing shopping, cooking, and cleaning. After we kids did our chores, we headed out to play. Once outside, Saturdays were actually pretty fun. During the ten years we lived across the street from my grandparents, every Sunday was exhausting. The day started innocently enough: the entire family filed into church like good little soldiers dressed in their finest clothes. After mass, we piled into the car and headed home for a family breakfast. Sadly, almost every Sunday our home turned into a war zone. As we kids cleared the breakfast dishes, our parents began their weekly ritual of fighting. First a criticism, then a sarcastic response or disgusted scowl, and my mother would take offense. My parents' fight escalated within minutes to a crescendo of raucous screaming, slammed doors, and swearing. It usually lasted for hours; I'd hide in my tiny bedroom closet amid shoes and clutter and read or do homework. If my reading and homework were both done, I joined my brothers and sisters in front of the television. With the family room door closed behind us, we attempted to drown out the uproar as they moved their fight from kitchen to bedroom to basement. We couldn't find solace outside or at a friend's home because we knew the rule: "Sunday was family day," so none of us could leave. We were trapped. For the five of us, family time was trying to find a way to escape the insanity. Hours of fighting routinely ended when my father surrendered with an insincere apology and withdrew in defeat for a nap on the living room couch. We stayed clear of both parents. Walking on eggshells, we knew the ceasefire could erupt into another explosion if we stirred the still-smoldering flames of the battle.

I remember being terrified that a friend would stop by one Sunday to play and hear the fighting. That never happened, so it remained my shameful secret. This would be just one of so many shameful family secrets that shaped my life. I assumed that this fighting wasn't normal for most families, but I had absolutely no idea what normal was. All I knew was I hated that chaotic rage and as an adult I wanted no part of it in my married life.

My Family

After all of those years of Sunday fights and weekly clashes, there I was trying to create my own family. I found myself sharing that cozy kitchen with my husband, feeling trapped once again in a scary cycle of conflict, yelling, and hurt feelings. The idea of allowing the development of the exact same battleground I had endured as a kid was absolutely unacceptable! I loathed that family hostility and could no longer survive in that insanity. I had to do something completely different. Completely opposite. I made some phone calls, and we did the unthinkable—my husband and I sought out marriage counseling. Counseling was taboo in the 1980s, so secretly, over the course of a couple of months, we met with our counselor every week. While my husband's parents lived out of the country and we had very limited contact with them, he had not yet dealt with some of the issues he had faced growing up. This gave us an opportunity that neither of us had ever had: self-discovery. We explored birth order and identified our individually assigned childhood roles in our families. We saw how those patterns could continue into our marriage. We discovered the emotional damage of confusing childhood messages. We learned how our childhoods and family patterns set us up for our fights, and we gained valuable insights and learned new and healthy approaches to conflict. Knowledge is powerful, and slowly our miscommunications no longer erupted into fights. Our newly acquired communication skills actually worked. I felt so empowered. I was hooked. Self-awareness and making conscious choices were new concepts, and that was exciting. Counseling introduced me to a world of choices in which I could create my own life with intention and purpose. I didn't know it then, but those skills would serve me well in the future with my family of origin. For the time being, my reactivity and my husband's anger calmed. In addition to improving our interaction, counseling provided me insight on the importance of healthy boundaries. As I became more emotionally healthy and confident, I learned that my parents and siblings were neither normal nor healthy. In just a few years I would find out just how sick they really were.

But at the time, with new life tools and a better relationship, everything was truly falling into place, and our hope to have a child turned into the miracle we dreamed of. After a tiring nine months, I became a mom. This child was beautiful and precious—delighting me every day with a coo, mesmerizing eye contact, and a smile. I felt love like I had never felt in my life. I absolutely adored being a mother.

My child was perfect, and motherhood was amazing, but strange hints of an obscure fear began to develop as my baby grew into a toddler. My new boundaries with my parents were becoming especially important. They often dropped by our home unannounced, frequently waking the baby or interrupting our scheduled plans. They felt completely entitled to visit whenever they wanted. They even expected me to help run errands for them or clean their house! I was scared about enforcing new boundaries, but I didn't let them see it. With confidence and with the support of my husband, I stated exactly what I thought of their intrusive, selfish actions. I clearly outlined what was acceptable behavior. They became incensed and indignant. In a fit of rage, my mother screamed "I carried you for nine months, I bore you, and I own you!" I was speechless. Owned me? No one owned me, and no one would own my child. Infuriated by their attempt to control, I became aware of how incredibly unstable and unhealthy they truly were. Needless to say, as I maintained my firm, clear boundaries, their rage began to flow like a seething volcano. Their old standby reactions of fury vacillating with silent treatments began. When I refused to engage, their attempts at intimidation only escalated. We spent less and less time with the family, and my obscure fear turned into full-blown anxiety. After an active and deliberate search, my husband received a job offer that required us to move to a different city, twelve hours away. When I announced to the family that we were moving, my parents did not speak to me for weeks. During the two years after my child was born, I had used an inordinate amount of energy attempting to block their cruel attacks. I was exhausted. I could not get out of town fast enough.

With our home settled, we went about creating our life in this new town. My parents came to visit us only once, and the first question they asked was, "When are you moving back home?" The mood turned icy when my husband explained that we had no plans to return. I was enraged by the old verbal violence and subsequent silence they initiated in an attempt to intimidate me. After their visit, I became fiercely protective of our child and our little family. I would never allow them to be in a position to intimidate us again. Never. Phone calls kept a connection to my siblings and parents, but leaving my hometown had created an emotional distance. Interestingly, the longer I was away, the safer I felt. I thought I was feeling safe from my parents' judgmental criticisms and the insanity of the family dynamics, but there was more to it than that. I just couldn't put my finger on it. At least not yet.

Our little family returned only one time to my hometown for a family wedding, but I could not be bullied and controlled as I had been in my youth. We stayed in a hotel and chose our times to visit based on our preferences and our child's schedule. My healthy, adult boundaries infuriated my father. Yet under that anger I sensed a strange, growing panic. I could see it in his eyes. Was he afraid of my independence? My mother, on the other hand, was incensed by my resolve and strength. My refusal to return to my hometown left her exasperated. Family frustration escalated, but again I would not engage in their old, childish behaviors. After a couple of days of this abuse, my husband and I packed up our child and left early. Once again there were no goodbyes because my mother was maintaining her punishing silence. In solidarity, and with an eye toward self-preservation, my father joined in her silence. I would have none of it. We returned home. Months passed, and eventually communication was reestablished, but my boundaries and independence created a rift in the dynamics of the entire family, and it would never mend.

Leaving the dysfunction behind, my husband and I returned to living our own busy lives. We had not been to counseling for a few years, but when we were expecting our second child, tension started to build again. My husband's weeks of travel and his hyperfocus on his career created an imbalance of family responsibilities. I was a full-time mom and kept the family wheels turning. Plus, I was still working part-time evenings as a nurse in a local hospital. Pregnancy and being a single mom during the week while working evenings at the hospital left me exhausted. Fights over sharing the load erupted, so we tried what worked before. We found a new counselor. Her name was Jill, and she had a PhD in psychology. She was nice and helped us implement strategies to navigate the marriage stressors before the birth of our child. That was that. After about three sessions, we awaited the completion of our family.

Despite early labor and the need for a couple weeks of bed rest, we were thrilled to welcome another new baby into our family. Watching a newborn begin to smile and develop a unique personality is a miracle. We were over the moon with our little family and loving the interaction between siblings. As the weeks and months passed, sleep was becoming more regular, and life began to settle into a normal routine, as much as that is possible with a toddler and baby and bottles and boatloads of laundry. Regardless of the chores and responsibilities, life was good.

Changes Are Brewing

I thought everything was going well in our marriage and in our juggling act as parents. But a couple of months after my thirty-second birthday, I started to experience gradually worsening anxiety. There was nothing I could identify as a cause. I had experienced anxiety and even depression as a child–there had never been an obvious cause. I had been labeled a nervous child by my mother, but that didn't make sense to me then. This anxiety made no sense to me at that time. I tried keeping busy, which wasn't hard with a young family, but that didn't help. I couldn't shake it. I didn't yet realize that this anxiety was going to implode on me and the worst of the storm was about to hit. The dam in my mind, holding back the floodwaters teeming with shocking memories, was about to burst, and when it did, it would flood my very existence and leave a torrential wreckage in its wake.

When I was growing up in the '60s and '70s, there had been no discussion of childhood physical or sexual abuse except in cases so egregious they bordered on the severely pathological and made national headlines. No one thought childhood sexual abuse was common, and we certainly did not have the statistics we have now. Only in the last twenty-five years have we acquired excellent research and neurobiological science to explain that childhood abuse causes immense pain and suffering. The research and statistics also show that child abuse is far more common than originally believed. I was about to learn that first-hand!

I began to remember disturbing snippets of images with associated sensations of taste, smell, or feelings of pressure, choking, or an inability to breathe. The snippets evolved into full-blown memories. As the memories surfaced, I was shocked, terrified, and disgusted. I couldn't understand how those horrible visions could be real memories, mainly because I could not understand how I could have pushed them out of consciousness for so long into the recesses of my mind. I had no context for understanding. I wanted explanations. I wanted books with answers like I used to find in the library, but I was too busy trying to process what was happening to me. I didn't have the time or energy to go to the library, and we certainly didn't have a home computer with the Internet and its instant answers. As a teenager, I had seen the movie *Sybil* at the theater but thought it was confusing and weird. I remembered being intrigued when I watched Marilyn Van Derbur on TV talk shows in the early 1990s. She was the beauty queen, former Miss America, who had been sexually abused by her millionaire father and had split into a day Marilyn and night Marilyn. Intriguing, yes, but I could not personally relate to any of that, at least not until my memories burst through layers of denial. As my memories became very vivid, I realized I too had been sexually and physically abused. I was devastated.

Unfortunately just around the time that my memories surfaced, TV news shows and grocery store tabloids mocked the investigators of a handful of sensationalized sexual abuse cases. The theory of repressed memories became very controversial. A few poorly trained counselors led their clients to produce false memories that led to the clients accusing innocent people of horrific abuse. The damage was devastating to all involved. Those cases created suspicion and a terrible setback for those of us who were truly experiencing recovered memories. That controversy stung. It was painful enough to accept the abusive memories of my childhood, but when so much skepticism swirled around their validity, I was scared that others would not believe me.

It has been over twenty-five years since my first memory surfaced. I have spent all the years since reading everything I could on science and new research. I needed to understand how I came to remember my horrible childhood abuse when I turned thirty-two. I felt so lost in confusion and sadness. I drifted in that confusion, trying to find my way in the aftermath of what felt like a storm throwing bolts of memories from the sky. I will share some of what I have learned in my extensive search. I hope to be a bit of a navigator for you. I hope to steer your understanding of how memory protects children who are abused. Unlike me when I first began to recover my memories, survivors now have access to excellent peer-reviewed research and exciting neurobiology as a rudder so they will not find themselves lost and drifting in a sea of questions.

Fortunately, we now have a much better understanding of memory and how the brain protects abused children through complex mechanisms such as repression and dissociative identity disorder (DID). Jim Hopper stands out as a clinician and researcher who has studied the long-term effects of child abuse and used the internet to share important things he has learned. Dr. Hopper began offering web resources on recovered memories of sexual abuse in 1995. He wanted people to have access to quality scientific and scholarly work on traumatic and recovered memories. As you travel back in time with me through my childhood, you will understand that the mind of little Janey had to find a way to cope and forget the abuse that happened. Repression is the way my mind dealt with my abuse, yet it was not a complete and total amnesia, and it is now known that at least 10 percent of people sexually abused in childhood will have periods of failing to recall their abuse, followed by experiences of delayed recall. Dr. Hopper cites supporting research and states it is not rare for people who were sexually abused in childhood to go for many years, even decades, without having recognizable or explicit memories of the abuse, just as I did. People almost always have implicit memories of the abuse—that is, memories they did not realize were memories, such as physiological or emotional responses triggered by encountering things associated with the abuse, like a smell or being touched in a certain way (Hopper, 2017).

This exactly describes my experience. I had implicit memories all my life. While confusing, I rarely talked about them. It is awful to feel different, especially as a child. It is extremely unsettling to not understand what you are experiencing. Eventually, my implicit memories evolved into the actual or explicit memories when my denial crumbled. I was lucky I did not split like Marilyn Van Derbur. While integration of personalities is possible in therapy, it would have required even more work than I already had to do. According to the National Alliance on Mental Illness, DID (often referred to as multiple personality disorder) is characterized by alternating between multiple identities. A person may feel like one or more voices are trying to take control in his or her head. Often these identities may have unique names, characteristics, mannerisms, and voices. People with DID will experience gaps in memory of everyday events, personal information, and trauma (National Alliance on Mental Illness, 2017).

Thankfully, with clinicians like Dr. Hopper and highly respected organizations like the National Institute of Mental Health (NIMH), the Centers for Disease Control (CDC), and the National Alliance on Mental Illness (NAMI) acknowledging the high incidence of childhood abuse (one in four girls and one in five boys), and more accepted understanding of how the brain processes memory, we no longer have to debate the validity of repressed memories and DID, and instead we can focus all of our efforts through education and awareness on helping survivors heal and preventing children from being abused.

My New Reality

When, one day at the age of thirty-two, I remembered my abuse, my life was moving along just like any other day. When I started to notice those disturbing clouds of anxiety off in the distance, I tried to keep busy and assure myself that the sky was just fine, just like any other day. But soon those gray clouds of anxiety began to billow into a menacing dark panic I could no longer deny. The winds whipped snippets of gross and disturbing sights before my eyes, but it was all so dark and confusing, and I couldn't make sense of it. Suddenly the sirens started to wail, and the winds of memories started to explode around me. I could barely catch my breath in the dust of the winds when another memory and another and another relentlessly pummeled me to the ground. I couldn't tell what I was experiencing because the explosion of all the repressed memories roared through my life with a terrifying, thunderous howl. I grabbed onto others' hands and listened for their direction, and I cried in fear and confusion. Weeks of deafening winds, pelting hail, torrential rain, and horrible debris exploded around me. And then I realized that, just as suddenly as it had begun, the storm had passed and I had survived. The worst was over. I emerged from the storm to assess the damage, and it was devastating. Nothing was the same. I was dazed and frightened. All the old familiar sites were gone. Everything I grew up with had been destroyed. The family I grew up with had deserted me. Bruised and sore and nursing wounds, I stood with my small children and tried to see light through the clouds. As I stumbled through debris and tried to find a new path, those I called parents told friends and loved ones that I only imagined the storm and I was crazy because there were no winds or debris or pain or terror or loss. It never happened, they said. I heard them say I only pretended to be in a storm so I could collect money for imagined damages.

And as I tried to find a new home, a new reality, a new life, I realized how very much I had lost. I had lost my childhood. I had lost any hope of ever having a loving mother or father. I would never be invited to another birthday or anniversary celebration with extended family, and there would be no family weddings, no invitations to baby showers, and no deaths to mourn or tears to shed for those who loved me well. I lost every sense of birth, death, and the natural order of life. The losses never lessen. Grief never ends. When asked about holidays and my hometown, I say I have no more family; they are all gone. And those words crush me with a loss so deep, so profound, and so painful that I must catch my breath before I can speak again. I must compose myself to continue my conversation. And I act as if my life is like everyone else's around me, but it is not the same. Nothing would ever be the same. I have no true, past family memories to hold onto, no fun stories to share with siblings, and no future trips with my clan. I am alone. There are no dots to connect my past to my present, no years to share as we all age, and no important life experiences to hear about. My life has profoundly changed, and nothing, absolutely nothing, will ever be the same. I will grieve every day for the rest of my life. And yet life must be lived, and my children must be nurtured and loved into maturity so I can watch them marry, build their lives, and have children of their own. And most importantly, my children are alive and safe. I've learned to live in the moment. There is nothing to draw me back as an anchor, no ties to my past. Nothing now but the moments I live and the future I dream. And so I hold the dichotomy of profound loss and joyful anticipation simultaneously as I move through this new life, one minute at a time.

Driving Home

On a dreary winter afternoon, the kids and I were heading home in the typical mom minivan after a busy day of school and work. Laughter amid stories and chattering about their day at school tumbled up from the back seat. As I sat at an unusually long red light, my mind started to wander. Just a year before, my life had been turned upside down.

I was jolted back to reality with a question that hinted of whining: "How much longer?"

"Soon" I responded.

"That's what you said before," my little preschooler mumbled. So much for calm reflection. I rubbed my temples and stretched my neck to release the knots in my shoulders. Again, my thoughts drifted as I remembered how I had been so determined in those few months after the first memory to stop all childhood abuse. That sounds so naive, but I had been determined to make a difference. I was somewhat melancholy as I realized I had done nothing but get on with life in the year since the exhausting memories flooded my mind. While I was more free and more energized because I was no longer using enormous amounts of energy to repress all of those memories of abuse, I still hadn't stopped the abuse of other children. I had made no changes. I had not written my book or even started it. A sadness and sense of failure fell over me, and then suddenly, I was surprised to "hear" a gentle whisper in my ear: "You have stopped the abuse for your children and their children, and you will write your book in time." The whisper did not originate from my own thoughts. The peace I felt with that encouraging message was overwhelming. It was as if God had been sitting right next to me and gently put His hand on my shoulder to encourage me. As I glanced in my rear view mirror at my beautiful, happy children, I realized that I really had stopped the cycle of abuse and that I would be reminded of that every time I looked at their beautiful faces. I had heard a whisper from God. If God was satisfied with me at that time in my life, then so was I. The green light was finally mine! I made my left turn. As I pulled up, I could see a brightly glowing, welcoming light flooding through our window. We were safely home.

I WANT TO TELL YOU A STORY

We hear of children being neglected, abused, and molested frequently in news stories and through social media. Usually the difficult and painful stories are told weeks or months after the abuse from a third person who has interviewed first responders, collected facts from social services, and pieced together the details of the police reports. The story is typically presented in a factual, journalistic news style. We often feel repulsed, enraged, and frightened because children are so vulnerable and helpless. But we can't help them, so we feel powerless. We hate to feel powerless, so with sad faces and shaking heads, we long for the next commercial or turn of the page. We seek to create distance in our minds and find emotional relief. We convince ourselves that child abuse is rare and only occurs in seedy hotels or by drug-addicted parents. We choose to believe that no such horror could possibly occur in our neighbors' homes or, God forbid, our own home. And that faulty belief allows child abuse to continue in every neighborhood and in every socioeconomic class. But I want you to know the reality of abuse. I want to help you. I want to tell you a story, my story. I want you to stand next to me as I endure the abuse you want to believe is rare. I want to show you that child abuse is, sadly, very common, but I will help you feel empowered instead of angry and helpless. I want to give you tools to help those small, hurting children who are so vulnerable. I want you to quietly stand near little Janey as she physically and emotionally endures her abuse, observe what she feels and how her mind works to cope, and make sense of the horrific insanity of her life. While my childhood was often terrible, it wasn't all horrific. Kids have to live and go to school, do chores, make friends, and play. You may smile as you read about the antics of my other, completely normal, childhood adventures. But remember as you travel with me through my childhood, Janey's stories may be chaotic and often painful to read, but I want us to share some common goals of increased awareness, hope, and intervention. You can choose to commit to supporting those children who pass through your life by recognizing signs of abuse. You don't have to shake your head and deny. You may actually be able to help. You may not always be able to pluck those children out of their situations of abuse, but your gentle kindness and availability may be the one ray of light that gives them hope and provides them a belief in goodness and love as they navigate their recovery later in life. As we go back in time and you travel with me through the abuse, focus on the little girl, not the abuser, so you will then feel empathy and hope rather than rage and despair. You may want to pick Janey up and run to safety but feel angry because you can't. Please trust me; I promise you it will be OK.

I Didn't Want To Be There Anymore

If you could stand close to the side of the refrigerator, you would have a perfect view of the small kitchen area and the crowded dining room where we huddled together for meals. It's hard to imagine fitting seven people at that table, but we did it all the time. So much noise and commotion, but I felt an eerie separateness from it all.

I was almost four years old. My mother stacked dinner dishes in the kitchen cabinets behind me. My older brother and sisters helped clean the tiny kitchen and carry dirty dinner dishes from the table. Mike was supposed to be cleaning up his Lincoln Logs. But he found it impossible not to secretly build one last cabin before all the wooden logs and red plastic chimneys disappeared back into the cardboard box. I hoped he wouldn't get spanked with the belt for not doing what he was told. I hated hearing his cries, or mine, when we got beaten, especially with the belt. Mom's slaps were wicked hard, and after multiple blows, we melted in tears. But if Dad got mad, it was the belt. Painful, red bottoms and twitching thigh muscles accompanied screams and cries of terrified pain. I hated the belt. I wonder if anyone ever saw those marks.

I listened to all the clinking of dishes and chatter within the room. The sounds echoed as if they were far away. My mother gave orders, and as usual, she found fault with every forgotten crumb or, God forbid, someone touching clean dishes with hands that had touched the dirty ones. Anthony and my sisters, Jenny and Debbie, began to argue over whose turn it was to wash or dry. This irritated Mom, and she started yelling. "Dammit, you lazy kids are driving me crazy! For once, just shut up and do your chores without fighting!" I lay on my tummy at the top of the steps, peering down into the basement. My little cotton striped shirt and brown corduroy pants did not soften the linoleum beneath me. I could hear the muffled voices of my father and grandfather in the basement. As I lay calmly at the top of the stairs, I could see the support column at the bottom of the wooden steps. My mom always warned us to be careful at the top of the stairs and hold onto the railing because if you fell down those steps, you would hit that column and crack your head open and die. Mom complained of the post's placement in the line of the stairway and its looming danger of death every time anyone opened the basement door. I don't know what I thought dying was. All I saw were cartoon characters dying, growing angel wings and halos, and flying up to the sky. Bambi's mother got killed, and Bambi was so sad, I cried. That was dying. As the dishes clanked behind me, I felt disconnected from all of the noise. Sad and alone, I felt a familiar, scary feeling as I heard my dad's voice. As Mom began to scold Mike for playing with the Lincoln Logs, I slowly inched my body over the top step, and with one big push, I shoved myself off the stairway, tumbling head over heels. I could feel the banging of the edges of the wooden steps as I tumbled, and while it hurt, my head missed the support beam by inches and my goal was unmet. As if in slow motion, I could faintly hear my mother scream for my father. As I was just about to crash, my father jumped in front of the post and caught me in my midair tumble. He scooped me up and ran up the stairs with me. What had just happened? I was not supposed to be there. It was all a blur. My mother grabbed me in her arms. How did Dad actually run and grab me faster than I could hit the post? As I stood on the bathroom toilet lid, my mother sprayed Bactine on the abrasions on my arms and washed off the cut on my head. I was crying. She told me it would stop hurting soon. But I was really crying because something didn't work. I was so confused. I wasn't sure why the urge to hit the column was so strong. I just knew that I didn't want to be there anymore. And I still was.

The dishes were washed and dried. Anthony swept up crumbs from under the table. Jenny and Debbie examined my bandages as Mike continued cleaning up his Lincoln Logs. I felt very lonely, and that terrible, scary feeling that I would later learn was anxiety washed over me as I heard my father's voice. I sat next to Mike and watched him as he pretended to put away his little plastic logs. My bumps and bruises hurt. I was still Janey, still in that house, and still nearly four years old. Maybe if I had pushed off those steps a little sooner, I would not be there watching Mike build his last fort. Why did I push myself off the steps? I couldn't remember at that point. But I eventually would, and I'm going to tell you of a terrible childhood that had already led me to the point of wanting to be gone rather than trapped in this life with these people who called themselves my family.

GOD GIVES CHILDREN ANGELS

What could have started such a lonesome and sad childhood that I felt compelled to find a way to "not be" anymore? It started very, very early. Let me take you to the day when I remembered the agony and terror. I could not use words to explain because I was only twelve weeks old.

No one ever knew because I was too embarrassed to admit it, but as a child my hands always shook and my heart raced whenever I heard the loud rush of water filling a bathtub. Who feels like that for no reason? You'd have to be crazy, but years later it would all make sense. My husband had turned on the water to fill the tub for the kids to take their nightly baths, and I was bringing in fresh towels. Life was beginning to settle after the explosion of memories, but occasionally something triggered a feeling, then a panic, and then bursts of images that led to a memory. However, this time was unique. There was a trigger and panic but no images, just sensations and awareness.

Suddenly the sound of the water filling the tub roared in my ears. In my already hyperalert state, I began to cry. This time I didn't just have shaky hands. This time I was filled with terror. It was evening, but I called Jill, my psychologist, on the phone through the answering service, and she quickly called back. I sat alone on the floor of the closet and told her I was remembering something, but I didn't know what I was remembering. Her instructions were the same as they had been before: in order to detach my emotions from the memory, she told me, I would need to explain the memory as if I were watching it on a TV screen. That was difficult to do this time because I was only sensing things. She told me to tell her what I was feeling. I was so upset and crying, but I was able to explain that I sensed human body warmth and the smell of a familiar person and quiet darkness. Suddenly that warmth and quiet were snatched away. I was shocked by a harsh, bright light. The terror intensified as I heard a rushing sound, and it was getting louder. I began to sob. I suddenly felt searing pain burning between my legs. But it wasn't between my legs that felt it; it was just me that felt it. I was the pain. I was the world and the world was pain—scorching, terrifying, and scalding pain. The rushing sound stopped. The searing throbbing didn't. I couldn't escape the horrible, shrill screaming. I was the pain. I was the scream. That smell and feeling of being held by the "familiar" tried to slip in, but the pain was overpowering. I became aware of a presence different from the familiar smell. That presence would later visit in the worst of the abuse. God gives children angels in their terror and shock. I don't know how I know this, but I do. I experienced it. A beautiful, gentle, heavenly presence of Light held me as I throbbed in pain and fell into shock. That heavenly presence would be my comfort in the weeks to come as I endured the pain of having raw, blistered skin cleaned after soiled diapers. That gentle presence never left me and still is a sweet comfort in times of great fear and sadness.

As I grew older, I remembered Mom's disparaging remarks about a pediatrician who had prescribed diaper rash cream for me when I was twelve weeks old. Mom frequently told a bizarre story that always ended with her being the protector and savior. We listened as we sat around the table eating breakfast or while Mom lamented about how hard it was to raise us kids. The story was always the same. She took me to a doctor when I was an infant. He was a horrible doctor because he had given her diaper rash cream and it had caused second- and third-degree burns on my bottom. As the story went, the pediatrician took one look at my inflamed and blistered skin and wanted to immediately admit me to the hospital, where nurses could take care of my burns around the clock. But Mom said she grabbed me off the exam table, bundled me up, and ran out of the doctor's office. She bragged about how well she took care of me and then puffed with pride when she said no one could ever take care of me in the hospital as well as she could at home. The story never made sense to me, and I always felt scared when she spoke about it.

As the diaper rash story became part of family lore, it never made sense how a cream prescribed by a doctor could cause second- and third-degree burns. It never made sense to me why my mother wouldn't let someone take care of me in a hospital. I asked her those questions when I was about eight. Mom erupted into an explosion of rage, slamming her hand on the table as she screamed, "I love you more than anyone in the world. No one could ever take care of you like me!" I jumped in my seat at the table and tears welled up in my eyes, but I did not cry. The story was repeated many times during my childhood. It still made no sense, but I never asked any other questions. After my terrifying call with Jill, all my questions were answered.

In a counseling session later that week, Jill explained that you can have memories in the preverbal period of infancy. Memories can still be intact despite the fact that an infant obviously lacks the necessary language to report the abuse. As an infant, I had no concept of separateness. I was the world. I believe the horrific pain associated with rushing water was embedded deep inside my soul, so it finally made sense why that sound triggered panic. I wasn't crazy. As I later gathered more research, I learned that abuse during infancy has a profound impact on the baby's brain and emotional stability, but sadly, most traumatized infants end up "remembering" the trauma in one way or another for the rest of their lives (Farley, Loveless, Palusci, & Taroli, 2014). If Mom had not repeated the story so many times over the years, I may never have had any context for my rushing-water panic. Fortunately, her diaper rash story, which was filled with lies, ultimately led to my truth.

Electric Train

Christmas is one of my favorite holidays. I love the decorations, wonderful treats to eat, carols on the radio, and spending time with family. So it never made sense that one toy often found under a Christmas tree would bring about feelings of rage and hatred. A dark, cruel act revealed the entitled and twisted nature of my father and brother. It was a dark, cold, blustery winter evening. The little house we lived in had a chill no matter how much the furnace was meant to warm the rooms. I sat coloring at the kitchen table when Mom put on her coat. She was getting ready to leave with my brother Mike and my sisters. My eyes welled with tears. I jumped from my chair and threw my arms around Mom's legs, begging her not to leave. She laughed, and my siblings shook their heads at my silliness, but I hated staying home alone with my dad. Mom laughed and called me a momma's baby as my father picked me up to allow them to leave. I wiggled myself out of his arms and ran to my room. I was terrified but didn't know why. Sitting alone on my bed, I heard the front door click shut behind my mother. I jumped up and peered out my small bedroom window. My heart sank as I saw the car driving out of the driveway, and I watched as it turned out of sight. Panic. Terror. Dad entered my room with an evil smirk on his face and picked me up. I could hear myself screaming as tears rolled down my flushed cheeks. I unsuccessfully struggled to break free from Dad's tight hold as he walked down the steps into the basement. I hated the basement. I hated it. As we descended into the dim lighting, I saw a plywood table supported by sawhorses. On that table was my brother's new electric train, set up in a circle. The green painted wood and small plastic trees and little houses created a village scene around the tracks. The train moved along the tracks as Anthony pushed the plastic control lever on the square power box. Wires from the track ran to the box. I could see them as my father strategically set me on that table. I fought my father's hold as they both tied me with rope and a couple of old belts to the sawhorse legs, and then for added insurance, they tied my arms above my head to a main support beam. I could barely move, much less escape. I could not believe what my brother did next. I screamed, "I'm telling Mom!" as Anthony yanked off my pants and underwear and pulled my legs apart and secured them with more twine. Anthony's mouth curled into an evil smile as he cupped his hands together near my face, revealing the white fur and pink red eyes of a mouse, its nose twitching and its tail dangling through his fingers. He disconnected the set of wires from the train tracks while leaving the other ends attached to the power box. With his thumb and finger he pried the mouse's jaws open and shoved the electric wire into the tiny mouth. Dad turned the lever of the power box on, and I heard a shrill squeak and saw the joy and thrill on their faces as the mouse suddenly stopped moving. They laughed with wicked, cruel delight. Anthony threw the dead mouse across the basement floor. I cried in fear and sadness. I felt as helpless as that mouse. Anthony then took the same wires and pushed them inside of me in between my legs. The sharp metal scratched as the train tracks beneath my struggling body dug into my skin. Dad's hand went toward the electric control box just as it had moments earlier. I stopped crying, I could barely breathe. I was going to die just like the mouse. From that moment of terror, I was completely dissociated. I could hear their voices and found myself watching everything unfold from a distance. A shock from the wires jerked me back to awareness. I cried out in pain and fear, but I immediately realized I had not died. Anthony and Dad were mocking me in laughter, continuing to call me a baby as they loosened the ropes and belts. Before the final rope was released, Dad bent over to my ear and said, "Don't you ever tell, or someday I'll come for your kids." I had no idea what he meant. My kids? I was a child, a little girl. With the last knot untied, I felt the track scratch my back as I scrambled off the table. I left my pants and underwear behind. Their laughter faded as I ran upstairs. I quickly reached my bedroom and put on my pajamas. Rocking back and forth in bed, I was crying and clutching my doll. Within a matter of minutes the memory became foggy and was soon lost. I still felt terrified but did not know why I was so frightened. The tears began to dry as I fell into a light sleep; the slamming of car doors outside woke me. I jumped from my bed and ran to Mom and hugged her tightly. She laughed and again told me I was a momma's baby. Maybe she was right. I was so afraid when she left and was incredibly relieved they got home. I had no recollection of the train, mouse, electric shock, humiliation, or fear of death. The intensity of my panic and crying when she left and relief when she returned made no sense, so I thought she must be right: I was just a baby. I felt so confused, but the voices of my sisters as they unpacked groceries grounded me a bit, and I was soon brushing my teeth and getting ready for bed. Confusion and fear lingered as I recited my bedtime prayer with Mom and Dad, and I soon fell asleep.

My Two Moms

That spring we had a cold spell after several beautiful, sunny days; it was hard to have to wear a jacket again. It was very chilly on that late spring morning. The other kids were off to school already, and it was just Mom and me in the kitchen. I wanted to watch cartoons. It's not uncommon for three-year-olds to be a little picky with their food. I was no different. I wasn't at all hungry as I stared at the cereal floating in the milk in my bowl. With my spoon, I pushed aside the flakes as if they might disappear with my uninterested strokes. I told Mom I wasn't hungry. I jumped when she snapped that I needed to eat. Why did I need to eat if I wasn't hungry? I took another bite, but the full bowl continued to loom before me. I tried to take one more bite but couldn't get the spoon to my lips and dumped it back into the then-soggy cereal. I told Mom again that I didn't want to eat because I wasn't hungry. Mom's face contorted, and she shrieked my name. My regular mom disappeared and the bad, enraged mom showed up. I jumped in fear, but I had no time to run. Mom grabbed me by my little arm as I started to fall off the chair. Mom dragged my little body out of the kitchen, and I began to cry, but there was no response from this terrifying, raging woman who was no longer my regular mom. I felt like a rag doll as she dragged me into the bathroom. "You don't want to eat?" she asked, screaming. "You ungrateful brat. You'll eat when I tell you to eat." The toilet was full of feces. Someone had had diarrhea and had not flushed it away. Suddenly, as violently as I had been jerked from the chair, Mom lifted the seat and screamed, "You'll eat," and she shoved my tiny face in the toilet bowl. I screamed as I felt my head submerge into the water of filth. The stench and taste gagged me as my head was plunged again and again into the disgusting water and my head hit the porcelain bowl. Finally, mean Mom pulled me up straight, and with eyes filled with disgust and rage, she said nothing and turned and walked out of the bathroom, slamming the brown wooden door behind her. I stood in shock and started to cry. I must have done something very bad. I wanted my mommy but not the mommy who had just left the bathroom. I tried to turn the bathroom doorknob, but my hands were too small and wet, and I wasn't sure what I would encounter, or whom. I slid down the door and sat on the floor, still crying softly. I tried to wipe my face with my dirty little fingers, but my hair dripped with feces. I cried, "I'm sorry, Mommy." I was trapped in the bathroom—shaky, filthy, smelly, and wet. The taste in my mouth gagged me. "I'm sorry, Mommy." My salty, wet tears and snotty nose only added to the filth.

Slowly the door of the bathroom began to open, and it pushed up against my little body. Terror flooded over me. I could not move. I could barely breathe as Mom entered the room. Her face was calm, and her eyes grew wide as if she didn't know how I came to be such a mess. Mom said, "Oh, Janey, what happened? Did you fall into the toilet?" I stood in shock and confusion, motionless. She gently lifted off my feces-stained shirt and then my dirty, wet pants. She picked me up gently and stood me in the tub. After she rinsed my hair and most of the filth washed down the drain, she closed the drain and lovingly held me as I sat in the tub filling with warm, clean water. I said nothing as she calmly and gently shampooed my hair and washed my body with a warm washcloth and Ivory soap. Tears rolled down my face. Mom told me she was so happy I didn't get hurt when I slipped in the bathroom. My hair and face and body were clean, but my mouth still tasted of the diarrhea I had been shoved into. I did not dare say a word. That hateful, enraged mom had been so crazy and terrifying, I didn't want to say anything to provoke her return. As she dried me off with the towel, my tears began to subside. I left the bathroom and went into my room to find my doll as Mom collected the dirty clothes and went down to the washer in the basement. I understood nothing except that I knew I might have done something wrong. As I dressed my doll and played in my room, I couldn't remember why I had taken a morning bath. We always took our baths on Saturday evening. As far as I can remember, I never ever complained again that I wasn't hungry. I always ate what was in front of me. I was happy when the other kids got home from school.

FIRST NEAR DEATH EXPERIENCE

The insane rage was not my mother's alone. There was a fact I knew since I was very little. Don't get in Anthony's way. He was always angry and cruel. All of us siblings knew he could lash out at any moment, and the most dangerous times were when he could get you alone, even if for a second.

When I was almost four years old, my parents decided to open up the wall from the formal dining room, creating a larger kitchen and adding more space for the table. For a small child, there was much excitement with the hustle and bustle of my grandparents being at our house for the weekend while my grandfather helped my father knock out drywall and studs and rebuild the opening to the kitchen.

Sawdust was everywhere, along with loud and interesting tools. It was so much fun! There was a lot of work done that weekend, and everyone seemed pleased with their efforts.

It was a Monday in the early summer, my grandparents were gone, and Dad was at work. Now that the carpentry project was completed, my sisters swept the remaining sawdust into piles and threw it in the trash. The refrigerator was the last appliance that needed to be moved into its new space. Debbie and Jenny were out back, and Mike was in the living room watching TV. Anthony, my mother, and I were in the kitchen. At thirteen years old, Anthony was already six feet tall, and he towered above his classmates. Anthony was intimidating, and he knew it. Always mean and sullen, he taunted and teased me unmercifully. My mother ignored my protests, saying, "He teases you because he loves you." It didn't feel like love. It felt painful and hateful. He called me "fat" names and often quietly repeated a chant of "Jane the pain." If he made me cry, he smiled in victory. The verbal insults were difficult, but Anthony's behavior was made worse because he was also calculating and a liar. He knew how to time his physical threats and abuse so he was rarely caught in the act, and he lied his way out of most situations with a polished assertion of innocence. Just out of sight from other family members, he was cunning and knew exactly how and when to execute his plans. I think he believed he was scaring me enough that I didn't tattle about all the abuse he inflicted, but in reality I just didn't remember. At least not yet.

Anthony and I were sitting at the kitchen table with Mom when she announced she was going to walk down to a neighbor's house to see if she could borrow a couple of eggs. Before she left, she told Anthony to clean out the refrigerator, toss out old food, and wipe down the shelves before she got back. She told him she wanted a clean refrigerator when they pushed it back into its new spot in the renovated kitchen. He hated chores, and there was a constant battle in our home because he despised being told what to do. That day was no different. He was angry and indignant, and I knew it. I usually stayed clear, but I wanted to see all the food that ended up on the kitchen table and see what would land in the trash. I should have known better. I stood by quietly. I watched as Anthony removed all the food and shelves from the refrigerator. I was surprised he was moving so quickly when suddenly, and without warning, Anthony grabbed me and threw me into the refrigerator and slammed the door behind me. It was dark, and the plastic walls were hard. The metal bins on the refrigerator door began to feel cool and poked into my back. I yelled at him to open the door. I pushed and pushed and began to panic. I tried to push really hard one last time, but the door wouldn't budge. I tried to position myself so that my back was against the door and my feet were pushing against the back wall of the refrigerator. If I could just get enough push with my legs, I might be able to shove the door open. I was just too little. My little legs and body frame were not long enough or strong enough to open the door. I then felt as if I couldn't get enough air, and I began to cry. I was terrified. It was dark, and he was mean, and it got harder and harder to breathe. I couldn't even yell. My chest heaved for air but there was none, and the darkness of the refrigerator slipped into blackness. Suddenly, I began floating. I could actually see my brother standing with his back against the refrigerator keeping the door shut, his defiant arms crossed tightly over his chest. I could feel his excitement. He felt in control and loved his secret that I was trapped inside and no one knew. Jenny walked through the back door and walked to the sink to get a drink. I could feel Jenny's fear. She knew something was wrong, and her thoughts focused on how to get back outside without making Anthony lash out at her. Setting her unfinished water glass on the counter, Jenny scurried outside again, unaware that I was in the refrigerator. I could feel her heart racing. She was relieved to be moving back out the door to the safety of the yard. I felt Anthony wondering why I had stopped trying to push the refrigerator door open. He wasn't feeling much excitement or having fun anymore. As I floated above I saw all the food sitting on the table, but I also saw a beautiful Light very far away, and I so desperately wanted to see it, but I suddenly fell out of the refrigerator as Anthony yanked the door open. I hit hard on the floor and gasped for air. Anthony grabbed me by one arm and pulled me away as he hurriedly began to wipe down the doors and shelves. He was still angry. I sat up slowly, feeling tired. My head was throbbing, and I was cold and trembling. I took big gulps of air until I felt strong enough to stand. Anthony grabbed me hard and said, "If you ever tell, I'll come find you when you get big and hurt your kids." Then he ignored me as if I did not exist. What did he mean? I couldn't understand what "your kids" meant. I stumbled outside and sat on the warm wooden steps. I could hear Mom walking up. She passed me as she walked up the back steps with eggs in her hands. I could hear her yell at Anthony for not finishing his job. I didn't know why I was so tired or cold, but I was warming in the sun. I looked toward the swing set. It might be fun to soar, so I left the yelling behind, sat on the metal swing, and pumped my legs, flying higher each time. I thought to myself that the day was going to be a very hot day.

THE BODY RESPONDS
WHEN WORDS FAIL

What happens to intrinsic memories that you can't remember? They have to come out somehow, but if you have no memory of them, your body often expresses what your words can't. That is how we ended up at the pediatrician's office one morning.

School was still keeping the older kids away, so the house was quiet. I often watched *Captain Kangaroo* and *Corky the Clown*. Cartoons were my favorite, and when *Casper the Friendly Ghost* came on, I scooted myself right up to the old black and white TV and became mesmerized. How much fun it would be to fly and be dead and yet still be alive! But poor Casper had to prove he was a good ghost because he was what he was, a ghost. I felt jealous of and sorry for

Casper every time I watched the cartoon. I wanted to be free and fly, but I knew what it felt like to be laughed at and feel so lonely.

    Our house was sparsely furnished, but I didn't know we were poor. I loved to run my fingers over the diamond pattern in the old green couch. The little old side table next to the armchair became my cash register when Mike and I played store. I used the small pullout drawer to hold the pretend money. I sold cans of peas or boxes of Jell-o to imaginary customers and bagged the groceries and sent them off to their hungry families. My doll Nancy Jones was a common customer as I propped her against the couch. I also held her tight when I didn't feel good. Everything seemed normal in our little house with many children. Everything appeared in its place, but appearances can be deceiving, and the deception in our home was so insidious that it sometimes leaked out in ways that only a physician might understand. But sadly, he didn't.

    One morning after watching *Casper*, I got a scared, funny feeling. That feeling would wash over me at any time on any day, and I never knew why. I would double over in pain and cry that my tummy hurt as I clutched Nancy Jones. The intense, spasmodic cramps could last a couple of hours or all day. After this episode of crying with stomach pain, I must have frightened my mother, so she called her sister to drive us to the doctor's office. Mom later told me she thought I had cancer because the spells would be so severe, and they never seemed related to anything I ate. I cried in pain on the drive to see Dr. Jacob, our new pediatrician. I had only been to see him once for shots. The only time we ever went to the doctor was for shots, which I hated, or if we were really injured or bleeding. I didn't need a shot, and I wasn't bleeding, but there I was in his office. Dr. Jacob was a sweet, gentle, white-haired man. The cleanliness of his office and the caring nurses in their clean white uniforms made me feel safe. By the time I got to Dr. Jacob's office, my stomach cramps had begun to subside. His nurse took me into the office, and he examined my tummy and listened to my heart and lungs. He found nothing wrong. I was a completely healthy, normal three-year-old. I may have been healthy and normal, but my life was not. My mother was irritated that such pain could not be diagnosed, and her anger was palpable. I felt guilty that she spent money for the doctor, and I could not produce the pain for him.

Those horribly excruciating stomachaches plagued me into adulthood. They caused me to make several trips to the bathroom, where I would rock on the toilet until everything left my system. I would then go to my bed and lie on my stomach until I finally fell into an exhausted sleep. I would later awaken, feeling drained and soaked with sweat.

Whenever a school physical was required, my mother reported my continued stomachaches to Dr. Jacob. I often wondered about Dr. Jacob. Did it even occur to him that there might be something wrong in my life that led to such confusing bouts of pain?

My stomachaches became a part of the family culture—a guilt-producing frustration for me because they could prevent family activities or interfere with my mother's plans. I never felt normal because I could never figure out why those stomachaches came on so suddenly and lasted into adulthood. I hoped that every stomachache would be my last, but they only stopped years later when their cause was finally identified. The body releases the pain when the memories identify the cause. I wish my doctor had been more astute with his diagnosis or maybe more brave with his questions.

Sugar Cubes

My days revolved around playing with neighborhood kids, watching TV, playing with my dolls, and waiting for my brothers and sisters to come home from school. My mother watched *The Jack LaLanne Show*, and she did the same exercises he did. I just couldn't understand how you could do an exercise called a bicycle when you were lying on your back. But it was fun, and every morning we swirled, did jumping jacks, and touched our toes.

Dad was gone a lot because he was working late hours. Mom voiced her frustration often with Dad about his absence. She thought it was important to spend more time together as a family, so one day we all piled into the car and drove to his office on a Saturday morning. The closest I had ever been to a big office downtown was the one time we had gone to see the Christmas decorations in the storefront windows.

 I was excited but a little scared when we all loaded up onto the old, rickety elevator. First, a folding iron door with lots of diamond shapes was closed by my dad. Then the actual doors shut. We began to move up, and I was both thrilled and worried, but I didn't show it because my brothers and sisters all seemed calm and excited. I was relieved when the elevator reached the floor, the door opened, and my father pulled the iron diamonds to one side. I jumped out quickly, fearing it might spring back and close me in.

 The office was filled with desks, file cabinets, and desk chairs with wheels. I didn't know why Dad had to work so much, but Mom was happy because we were there as a family. Dad showed us the break room. They had a coffee pot and hot chocolate, and it was all free. I couldn't believe we could all have our own cup of cocoa. And those sugar cubes—I had never seen anything like them. I licked one, and sure enough it was sweet sugar. I popped it in my mouth and felt the grains of sugar melt as the cube dissolved and sweetened my tongue. It was wonderful. But the real treat was when Mike and I found the rolling desk chairs. We each lay on our tummies on the seat of a chair, got a running start, and then lifted our legs. The chairs flew down the shiny tile aisles between the desks. We flew like birds, giggling and laughing and even having races. Then the best game of all: one of us sat on the chair as the other spun it around and around as fast as he or she could, leaving the other squealing in delight. We both stood up laughing: dizzy, stumbling, and bumping into one another as we tried to walk. Mike and I were so entertained that I really didn't notice my older brother or sisters or my dad working at his desk. This was so much fun, and Mom was not getting after us like she usually did when we got so rambunctious. I was sad when we had to leave and couldn't wait to come back. We were allowed to take some sugar cubes home with us. We put the cubes in paper cone cups. I had never seen a cup like that before. I thought they were the silliest things I had ever seen. How could you set them on a table? But I had had too much fun to care. I happily and bravely walked into the elevator with the hinged diamond doors, and then the large metal door closed us all in. I was so enthralled with the funny-shaped cup filled with my very own sugar cubes that I didn't even notice that the elevator had stopped. My father opened the diamond-shaped metal doors. We all left the office, and I hugged the prized sugar close to me, wondering how long I would be able to hold out before I popped another in my mouth. I wanted that day, the fun we had, and my sugar cubes to last forever. But nothing good lasts forever.

I HATE RED PENCILS

The job my dad had at the office that was so much fun ended. I didn't know what being fired meant. I also didn't know why Mom was crying and why Dad was circling things in the paper and making so many phone calls. Within a few weeks, my dad was at another office downtown at another job and was working late into the evening. The summers in the Midwest were normally muggy and hot, and that night was no different. It was dark, and Jenny was asleep in the lower bed of the bunk bed right next to me, with Debbie in the top bunk. Our room was so small that we barely had enough room to walk between our beds. We often reached over and held hands. A small, blond, four-drawer dresser stood at the head of my bed. My twin sisters and I were eight years apart. Sometimes I was their little sister to watch over, and sometimes I was a pain in their neck, hanging around when they wanted privacy. They were much older and wiser eleven-year-olds. Their backs were turned to me as they slept facing the wall. I drew pictures with my finger on my wall. I could not sleep. It was not because the sweltering heat stifled my breath and not because I was so hot my sweaty neck and head stuck to my pillow. I was excited because my dad was bringing me a special surprise when he came home late from work. I was so excited, in fact, that I couldn't sleep. We were poor, but I didn't know that. We had clothes and a small house, and we always had food. We rarely got presents, and since Dad seemed to always be working late with his new job, it was exciting to know I would see him, but also doubly exciting that he was bringing me a surprise. I felt special.

I could see a dimly lit light in the living room. All five of us were supposed to be asleep. But I was unable to shut my eyes in my excitement and could hear Mom cleaning up a few last dishes and rattling around in our living room. Finally! I heard the car pull up outside, and my heart raced with anticipation since I knew Dad was home. It was dark, but I could hear his footsteps on the short concrete path as he headed toward the front door. A special surprise was soon to be mine, and I could barely contain my excitement. I heard Dad walk into the living room and the quiet voices of my parents. Within minutes I could hear him walking into my room. He knelt down and told me he had a surprise for me.

He pulled two red pencils from his pocket, and with the hall light on I could see that they were brand new. There were no teeth marks in the wood and no broken tips, and they even had erasers on the ends. I asked if they were all mine, and my dad smiled and said yes. I could smell smoke on his white-collared, short-sleeved work shirt and tie. Offices had no air conditioning then, everyone smoked, and the smoke gave him a musty smell. As I admired my red pencils and marveled that I did not have to share them, Dad pulled back the sheet covering me. Confused, I felt him pull up my thin nightgown, and without hesitation, he pulled down my cotton panties. I froze in disbelief as I clutched my pencils. Jenny and Debbie were asleep. I was alone. This didn't make sense. I dared not move, frozen in shock and fear. Dad began to lick between my legs. My legs were stiff, and I was holding my breath. I could not hold it long enough though. This could not be happening. He was completely silent as he knelt next to my bed and attempted to push my tight thighs apart. His hair was brushed sleekly back and his hairline was receding. In a horrid, raspy whisper, he croaked, "Don't you ever tell, or someday I'll come and find you and kill you and your family." Kill my family? Mom and the twins and Mike? I didn't think of Anthony. I was terrified, confused, and embarrassed. Something was wrong, but no words could come out of my mouth. It would have done no good. No eye contact was made, and he didn't even seem to know that this was me he was touching, licking, sucking.

The smell of musty cigarette smoke and old sweat sickened me. I tried to evaporate—to be nonexistent. The quiet licking noises suddenly stopped as I heard my mother yell at my dad in the loudest whisper she could utter. He jerked up and threw the covers over my naked bottom, my panties still pulled down to my ankles. Dad jumped to his knees, and I could hear angry, muffled whispers as Dad rushed passed Mom in the doorway. What had just happened? Why did he do that? As I lay still, frozen in my bed, I looked up to see Mom's face glaring at me in hatred. I felt so guilty. Something wrong had just happened, and it was painfully clear from the disgusted scowl Mom was shooting at me that I was to blame. Now what? I didn't tell, but was Dad going to kill everyone? I was terrified, confused, and sick with guilt. Mom abruptly left my doorway, and the hall light snapped off. I still held the two pencils tight in my fists against my chest. With my right hand, I pulled up my panties under the sheet and clutched the red pencils in my left. Fear, guilt, and shame flooded over me. I put the sharp red pencils into the space between the mattress and the metal frame. I rolled to my side. As I drew pictures on the wall with my finger, I forgot why I was still awake. I knew the red pencils were there, but I had no excitement or feeling for them. I felt anxious, guilty, and tired but wasn't sure why. My finger slipped gently down the wall in my last stroke of drawing my wall picture, and sleep mercifully carried me away.

I awoke in the morning and saw the red pencils between the mattress and bed frame and remembered Dad bringing them home. But I wasn't really interested in playing with them. I must have fallen asleep immediately after he put them in my hands because I couldn't remember how they got there. The morning was still cool, and I slipped out of bed to watch cartoons and wasn't very hungry that morning. I felt a little unsettled, but watching *Romper Room* shifted my attention, and I watched as my father drank coffee and as my mother cleaned off the kitchen table. It was a typical morning at the house. I couldn't shake the funny feeling I had, and I never knew why I felt it. But soon *Romper Room* had my full attention, and a new day had started. I would get dressed and eat breakfast. I wanted to play outside in the warm, sunny day. I never bought a red pencil in my life. In fact I hated them, which never made sense. To this day, even though I understand why I hate red pencils, I still can't bring myself to buy them or use them at work. A simple surprise turned into a horrible memory. I wonder how Dad weaseled out of that. Which Mom caught him?

HOP LIKE A BUNNY

As you have seen in my last few recollections, staying inside had dangers lurking in the dark, in secrecy behind closed doors, so I found it was usually best to play outside. I thought it was because I was freer to run and meet friends. But I was really never safe anywhere. Safety was an illusion. I was reminded of that fact the one cool summer morning when I was outside playing in the sandbox. We didn't have many toys, but after I sifted out the cat poop from all the stray neighborhood cats, I could build houses and draw figures in the sand. On a nice day, I could easily spend an hour with the sand and my imagination. That morning, lost in play, I was suddenly startled by my older brother standing over me. I pretended not to notice him even though my heart was beating so hard I could hear it pounding in my ears. Anthony was angry, as usual, and I knew something was not right when he grabbed me by the hand and jerked me up to my feet. I tried to protest, but he had a gun in his hand. It looked like the rifles that we saw in old Westerns on TV. I was scared. Was this going to be the time he killed me? I wondered what I did wrong and why he made me walk ahead of him. I dared not complain, but I wonder now why no one saw this little procession and tried to stop him. There was an open grassy field by our house. We walked through weeds taller than my soon-to-be four-year-old body. We continued until we were in the densest part of the field. No one would hear my scream over all the other playing, screaming children. Our neighborhood was overflowing with kids. I didn't have a chance, and I was shaking and beginning to cry. I begged Anthony to let me go home, and I wouldn't say anything to Mom or anyone, but he told me to shut up. He then told me to start hopping like a bunny. I started to cry. I was scared. As I opened my mouth with a plea to stop, Anthony put the rifle barrel in my mouth. I froze. I was going to die for protesting. Anthony told me if I didn't hop like a bunny, he would shoot me in the mouth and splatter my brains all over the field. I had no choice. I feared I was going to die one way or the other. I did what he said and started hopping. He yelled at me to hop higher. Just then I felt a burst of pain in my right bottom. It burned and started bleeding, but I wasn't dead, and I didn't think I was bleeding to death, but the blood and pain scared me. That's when I heard Anthony howling in laughter. The tears turned to sobs as I ran through the field toward home. His laughter was still loud and obnoxious, but I could tell that he was not following me. I ran in the house to my sister Debbie. By the time I got home I had forgotten what happened. She stood me on the lid of the commode and cleaned the area with soap and water. Debbie told me I was brave because it was still burning and the soap made it burn worse. We had Mercurochrome in the metal medicine cabinet, and she dabbed it on the wound. I began to cry. It stung so badly. But she said we had to get it really clean with medicine so it didn't get infected. I was crying from the pain of the wound. I was crying because of incredible fear, but I didn't know what I was so afraid of.

These were the times I felt different, crazy, or off because things just didn't make sense. I felt like all the pieces of my puzzle were not available. When Debbie asked me what had happened, I really didn't know, but I had to have done something. I told her I fell and there must have been a sharp rock or stick. Jennie came in, asked what happened when she saw me crying, and both of my sisters finished cleaning the wound so they could put a clean bandage on it. They helped me down and let me lay on the lower bunk bed. One sister stayed with me while my other sister went to the freezer and brought me a cherry Popsicle, my favorite. I knew I could get in trouble for eating in bed, but I didn't care. They were both being so nice, and I was finally able to stop crying. After I finished my Popsicle, my sisters told me to come watch television. I am sure they wanted to get my mind off of the pain and help me forget about my fall. My twin sisters were talking softly to each other as they walked to the living room. I could not hear what they were saying, but I did hear the name Anthony. I wondered later how many times they had known what had happened to me but kept the secrets guarded. Our bedroom was only eight feet wide. They had bunk beds, and I had a small child's bed. We could reach out and hold hands, so I can't imagine that the nights that my dad came in, they didn't see and hear something. Maybe if they said nothing then it wasn't real, or maybe if it was happening to me, then it wouldn't happen to them. I forgot what happened, but I don't know if they did. As I grew older and remembered the memories, I often wondered if they felt guilty or sorry. Maybe they didn't remember when they woke up in the morning. We were all victims in so many ways.

Years later, that BB would be seen on a full body X-ray prior to my back surgery. My doctor said, "You have a BB in your butt." I laughed at him and said, "I think I'd remember if I got shot by a BB gun!" Oh, how wrong I was.

THE WORLD IS A BIG, EVIL PLACE

While the bathroom had some horrid memories sometimes causing fear, that morning I felt safe. I used to love to sit on the edge of the bathtub and watch my mother put her makeup on. Often, after she was done washing her face and patting it dry with a towel, she told me she loved me, and then a mantra that I would hear over and over the rest of my life would commence: "Janey, the world is a big, evil place. Stay close to your family. They are the only ones you can trust. People you think are your friends will always hurt you." The tiles around the tub were smooth and cool. They were small, gray, and pink. The butterfly shower curtain made it look cheery.

As I sat on the tub that day listening to her, we must have been going someplace special because I had light peach pants on and a pretty flowered T-shirt. She was getting ready to go somewhere, and I was going with her. I listened to her words about the world being a big, evil place, never questioning the wisdom of such a statement. As she powdered her face, I suddenly slipped and fell butt first into the tub with my feet dangling over the edge. I was so shocked! I looked up at my mother, and she had a look of surprise too. I was waiting for something to hurt but it didn't. That was actually *fun*! I burst out laughing—and so did she. I decided one slide into the tub just wasn't enough. So I slipped and fell and laughed about four more times as she continued to put her makeup on, enjoying my antics. At that point, my world consisted of the joy of slipping in and out of the tub, giggling and laughing every time. I loved finding new games and moments of joy. That playful morning was one I cherished even though it was overshadowed by what I would later realize was such a depressing, dark message about people and the world.

I Felt Like a Movie Star

One Sunday afternoon, as was usual on the hot days of summer, a large number of people were standing in a neighbor's driveway, trying to find shade and making conversation. The houses were just too hot in the evening for us to stay inside. It was a common sight to see men drinking beer while their children played in the yard and mothers talked about whatever mothers talk about.

On that particular Sunday evening, I somehow got my hands on an empty jar that one of the kids had been waiting to fill with lightning bugs. When I grabbed it, he laughingly yelled for me to give it back. I started to run around the car with him chasing me. After about my third circle, I tripped on an uneven seam in the driveway and fell, with the jar breaking under my hand. I was just about three years old, and the amount of blood scared me. It hurt where the jar had cut open a portion of the inside of my left palm. My father came over and picked me up and was very angry. But as other fathers started to come close, he changed his expression and tone and acted as if he was concerned rather than annoyed. He took out the white handkerchief from his pocket and put it on my hand to stop the bleeding. It was a blur of pain and tears and Mom calling a doctor to meet us at an office near the house. I heard them talking about stitches as I sat in Mom's lap while my dad drove to some doctor's office in a little building close to our house. My parents had never taken us kids to him, but they needed someone close, and he was right around the corner. I was crying as much out of fear of stitches as I was because of the pain and fear of the cut. I had heard horror stories of kids getting stitches and how much it hurt. When we arrived at the office, a brown-haired doctor unlocked the doors and led us into an exam room. Mom was mad at my dad because he was supposed to have been watching me, so then Dad was mad at me. But that bickering stopped as we walked into the exam room. My hand was throbbing. I was afraid I was going to get in trouble for running with the jar, and I was terrified of stitches. The doctor cleaned my hand, and I held still as ordered. My tears were hot as they rolled down my face. But I knew not to move. He pulled out some gauze and two butterfly bandages. I couldn't understand why he kept calling them butterfly bandages—they didn't look like butterflies at all! But I didn't care because it meant I didn't have to get stitches. I melted into my mother's arms with great relief and held an ice pack on my hand to stop the bleeding. I had never been so happy to leave a doctor's office. Still being carried by Mom, we sat in the car and drove home. I could tell my father was still mad at me, especially since he had been obliged to pay the doctor for opening up his office and fixing my cut. I felt really guilty but really relieved that I didn't have to have stitches.

When we drove into the neighborhood and into our driveway, the car was suddenly engulfed by neighbors and friends, all cheering as if I had been pulled out of a terrible accident. Dad seemed to like all of the attention. I couldn't believe people really cared about me. I felt like a movie star! The guilt and fear were replaced with joy and shock by all the concern because I don't think I had ever felt that important. Every time I look at a bell jar or see lightning bugs, I look down at the scar, still barely visible on my hand. And I remember more of the celebrity feeling I felt than the pain or fear. Maybe I really was worth loving—at least it seemed like they cared.

Fourth of July Horror

I was turning five. July was a special time of year because it was my birthday month and you could legally watch fireworks on the Fourth. Outside, the smell of gunpowder was thick in the hot air, and firecrackers popped continuously throughout the neighborhood. It was too hot to eat inside, so for lunch we grilled hot dogs and made s'mores. My brothers and sisters and I played in the backyard, trying to stay cool and having fun with the neighbor kids.

Anthony found a small cardboard barrel with a lid on it that my dad had bought with some sort of supplies to do patio work. It was about three feet tall and about eighteen inches in diameter. Every box and container became an instant toy once it was discarded by adults. Some of the kids rolled down the hill in the barrel, and when they got out, hysteria and laughter filled the muggy summer air as they tried to walk straight up the hill, falling sideways every few feet.

After the other kids were called home to eat, Anthony was messing around with the cardboard barrel. I played in the sandbox, not paying much attention to him in the late, lazy heat of the afternoon. He innocently called me over, and before I knew it, he had taken the lid off the barrel and shoved me in it, slamming the lid on tight. I began to scream as I realized the barrel was filled with bugs of all kinds— crickets, grasshoppers, and beetles were crawling all over me and landing in my mouth as I screamed. I was hysterical and terrified. I tried to push the lid, but I was hitting the wrong end. I somehow got myself turned around, popped off the top, jumped out of the barrel, and began to run away from my brother. His skinny, pimpled face turned crimson as his hysterical laughter erupted. I ran as fast as my little legs could carry me to the front yard. I had spit out all the bugs while hot tears rolled down my face. I hated him for being so mean. I kept running, looking back to make sure he wasn't coming after me. I reached the front porch, sweaty and breathing heavily but unsure why I was so upset.

I sat on the cold concrete front steps, heart racing, wiping away tears I didn't understand. My friend Danny walked up and asked me why I was crying. I wasn't sure, but I couldn't say that. The words slipped from my lips. Jenny and Debbie wouldn't let me play with them. Danny was also the youngest in his family, so he understood. He asked if I could play, but I told him my mom was making dinner. I slid into the front door and walked into the kitchen. Anthony was sitting at the table with a strange grin on his face. I went into my room with my sisters. Every summer my brothers and sisters made fun of me when I cried and ran whenever I saw beetles and grasshoppers and crickets. It never made sense why I would feel so much fear of harmless bugs.

I'M SORRY, MIKE

Danny was my playmate. It was late summer and still very hot. Anywhere we could find cool concrete and shade was where we played. Mike, Danny, and I played ball on the driveway next to Danny's house. Danny's driveway had a cyclone fence and gate next to it that opened and closed between the two houses. The ball sailed over the gate, and Danny ran to go get it. He excitedly reached for the gate and when he swung it open, it hit squarely on Mike's forehead.

Danny stopped. I stopped. Mike gasped just before he screamed, and his eyes flooded with tears. In seconds, a huge goose egg the size of a golf ball formed on his forehead. I loved Mike and felt badly for him, but the goose egg made me want to laugh. I had never seen anything like that pop up on someone's head. Danny smiled, and my own amusement was tempered with fear that I would be blamed for Mike hitting his head. Someone had to take the blame in our home when something bad happened. I didn't want to get in trouble. I didn't want a spanking from Mom, and I sure didn't want Dad to beat me with the belt. Even though I was still afraid, I ran right behind Mike as he ran to our house next door and swung open the front screen door. Still howling as tears covered his face, Mike was stopped by Mom. She assessed the damage. Still afraid I was going to get a spanking, I tried to explain what happened, but between Mike's crying and Mom's crushing ice in a towel, no one could hear me. My sisters came out to see what was happening. Mom held Mike on her lap, holding the ice to his swollen head, while Dad got more ice from the freezer to add to the dish towel. His bump starting to turn red and then slightly blue and even began to subside as the ice stayed in place. I finally had a chance to explain, and I blurted out, "It was an accident; he got hit by the gate!" When I realized there would be no punishment, I was enormously relieved. I put my hand on Mike's leg and then took his hand in mine. As his tears faded, my fear melted. I quietly said, "I'm sorry, Mike." He was tired and closed his eyes as the ice relieved the throbbing. I sat on the couch quietly as Mom laid him down next to me and I held the ice to his forehead. He fell asleep on the couch. I felt like I was comforting Mike as I lay next to him and held his hand, and I too drifted off to sleep.

LIGHTNING BUG MAGIC

Anyone who has ever lived in or visited the Midwest during the summer has experienced the magical joy of lightning bugs. It was common to see families cooling off in the summer heat as the sun set and sparkles began filling the air. Kids loved them, and parents could relax because we stayed close and couldn't get hurt catching lightning bugs. They truly were enchanting. They floated effortlessly in the night sky like creatures from a fairy tale. We always saved a jar to create a lightning bug vessel. We poked holes in the lid for air because we knew all creatures needed air and we didn't want them to die. We added grass for food, and we started collecting. Which cousin or sibling could catch the most? My sisters were really good and seemed to be able to spot them just as the first flicker lit the air. You had to be gentle so you didn't squish them. Once you caught one between your hands, it tickled your palms, and we laughed with excitement as we put each in the jar. This ritual could last over two hours, and summer after summer, we gently captured these beautiful, floating creatures. Sadly and invariably, someone would hold one too tightly and it would become a lightning bug fatality, but there seemed to be hundreds floating in the air, so we would place the lifeless bug in the grass and remembered to be gentler if we wanted a glowing jar by the end of the night. Many summer evenings we planned to catch enough lightning bugs so we could drift asleep watching the twinkling in our jar. So many summer nights we planned to keep them alive through the winter by providing water, grass, and, of course, air, but invariably we awoke to find they had died. I always felt badly that I was the cause of their demise when I wanted them to last all year long. I was a seven-year-old child with a simple reality, but I eventually realized a creature that was this special could not be kept captive. I still remember the nights I fell asleep to their glowing and the peace it brought me. I remember many nights falling asleep with my jar of lightning bugs glowing in the darkness. For some reason, I never remember any of those special nights being ruined by an unwanted visit from my dad. For that I am eternally grateful. My lightning bugs were pure, and so were the nights I fell asleep with just them next to my bed.

PRIMAL INSTINCT

On a sunny but very chilly fall morning, Mom and I put on our coats and scarves and headed out the door. Since Dad usually took the car to work, we started our two-mile walk to the local grade school. Mom had a stack of papers to deliver to the teachers. I liked to walk, but this was a very long trek, and at three years old, my little feet got tired as I kept pace with my mother. After Mom dropped off the packet, we struck out for the return trip home. The bright sun and the crisp fall weather were wonderfully refreshing. The leaves were changing into beautiful hues of gold, burnt orange, and red, and the sun sprinkled through the branches as we walked along the streets. The amazing fall colors and fresh crisp air should have created a relaxing stroll with my mom, but soon I became very tired and begged Mom to carry me. Since we were almost there, she finally gave in to my pleas and picked me up. What a welcome relief to my tired little legs. The sun warmed my back, and the swaying motion in her arms lulled me into a calm, sleepy state. I rested my head on my mother's shoulder and could smell her familiar smell. I was startled awake by a fear that suddenly washed over me. Many years later, in therapy, I learned why I suddenly panicked in these situations. I could never let my guard down. But I had done just that as I snuggled into her shoulder. My vulnerability and her smell were triggers of intrinsic memories. Tears welled up in my eyes. As we turned the corner and I saw our house, I leaned my face into Mom's neck and bit her as hard as I possibly could. I did not let go until a sharp, sudden slap hit my bottom. My already fearful tears quickly turned to tears of pain, and I really began to cry. Mom screamed my name and roughly put me down to walk on my own, but only after I had received three more hard slaps to my bottom. As a child, I had no idea why these urges to bite took over so suddenly. All I knew was that an unexplainable, primal instinct of rage overtook me, and a scared, cornered animal lashed out from a false sense of safety. I never repressed these biting episodes, and they occurred frequently enough that it was often a family topic discussed after I grew up. As a child, however, biting my mom would remain one more confusing piece of my life that I could not understand. The cause of my biting was revealed much later in my life when all the pieces of my story were revealed. But that revelation was decades away from that sunny fall morning.

SECOND NEAR DEATH EXPERIENCE

I could take a bath by myself since at that point I was four-and-a-half years old. My mother checked on me to make sure I rinsed all of the thick, green Prell shampoo out of my hair. I felt very mature sitting in the warm water singing and playing with the shampoo lids and the cup we used to rinse our hair. In my world of imaginary waterfalls cascading from the cup into the warm bathwater, I barely heard Anthony walk into the tiny bathroom. I was now at an age where I felt funny having my sisters or brothers see me naked. Modest embarrassment was my initial feeling, but Anthony had a strange look on his face, and before I knew what was happening Anthony grabbed my arm, and in a sinister whisper he said, "You keep your mouth shut. You ever tell, and I'll kill you. Someday I'll hunt you down and, no matter how old you are, I'll kill you all." Kill us all? Who? But before I could think another thought, Anthony unzipped his pants and threw off his underwear. His penis was hard and red, and he was on top of me in the tub splashing water over the edge. I was terrified as he reached down and shoved my head under water, firmly holding me by my shoulders and trapping me inches below the water's surface. Everything was happening so fast. Holding my breath like I did in our little plastic pool in the summer, I felt Anthony moving up and down in the water until I felt his private parts touching mine. I knew this was wrong, but I was running out of air. I tried to struggle, but at fourteen years old, Anthony was already six feet tall, and as he leaned his body over mine, I was pinned by his weight and strength. My chest felt like it would explode, and I could hold my breath no longer. Bathwater rushed into my lungs. The burning, choking, and pressure in my chest exploded until I was gone. I no longer heard anything, and I realized that all the pain had stopped. I was completely calm as I drifted over the tub and watched Anthony press my limp body down as he continued to pump his naked hips over mine. I wasn't separated or dissociated from my body; I was dead. As I floated over the bathroom, I was surprised to see my face. I looked yucky. My eyes were wide open, staring straight ahead. My face was gray, my lips were blue, and my hair was floating straight out from my head in the water. I was not frightened but curious, as I knew Anthony's thoughts and feelings. Anthony did not know I had left my body. He was consumed with excitement, knowing that everyone was in the house but he could still do something so forbidden without anyone seeing him. He felt powerful, and the control intoxicated him. He felt no connection to me as a person, much less as his sister. His mind was singular. He was completely his own world. He didn't feel love or caring. He didn't feel fear. A connection to me or to others was simply not there. I watched from above as my body grew grayer and my eyes remained fixed and lifeless. In a split second, I was no longer floating above my brother. I was in a beautiful tunnel.

I was floating—then soaring and drawn toward this incredible, amazing Light. Beautiful, sparkling, multicolored lights grew even brighter as I drew closer and closer to the Light. It was the whitest and brightest light I had ever seen, but it didn't hurt my eyes. I couldn't reach it fast enough. Anticipation was exploding within me as I experienced an increasing power of love like I had never known. There were angels, but not like the pictures I had seen in my little church books. They were beautiful spirits of love, and they were completely devoted to the Light. Their songs were the most beautiful sound, unlike any music I had ever heard. In that instance of no time, I found myself in the presence of this intelligent, loving, beautiful reality, and the being of Light embraced me. I was still in the space of no time, no dimension, complete in this Light. I was just totally me, and

I was precious and adored by the Light. But then a horrible dimension entered this space. I was being pulled in two directions. As much as I could not fathom leaving this beautiful love of the Light where everything was real, perfect, pure, and safe, I felt pulled back. I was caught in a vortex. I no longer saw the Light, and I was suddenly slammed back into my body, lying on my side on the cold tile floor of the bathroom—naked, wet, and shivering. What had just happened? Confused and choking, gasping for air, I coughed my last mouthful of water as I raised myself up onto my hands and knees. Disoriented and shaking, I was suddenly terrified that Anthony might be near but didn't remember why I was so gripped in panic. I just wanted to get to my bed. I tiptoed into my room right across from the bathroom. I was shivering when I pulled on a shirt, some panties, and pants. I slid under the covers and slipped into an exhausted sleep for only a few minutes before I awoke to my mother's shrill voice yelling for me to pick up my bath towel. I didn't remember how or why I even got out of the tub, because I was supposed to stay in my bath until my mom came to help me dry off. While still scared and dazed, I also felt a very strange feeling, as if something good had happened. I felt a warmth, a peace, a love I had never known. Everything was still a bit hazy, but I got out of bed, threw my wet towel into the dirty laundry, and went back into my bedroom to dress my doll. I wrapped her in a blanket so she would be warm and safe.

SCARY AUNT JEAN

Riding in the car with Aunt Jean was scary. My dad took the bus so Mom could use the car to take my Aunt Jean to special doctors with my grandma. I didn't completely understand how you could be sick in the head, but that is what I was told was wrong with my Aunt Jean. Aunt Jean stayed at a big hospital. We would visit her outside in the big grassy area but never inside. I heard my brothers and sisters call her crazy. I never wanted to be crazy. I was terrified of ever looking or acting like her. My mom said she wasn't like the other kids when she was growing up. She always talked about feeling different. But she didn't act aggressive or bizarre until her late teens.

Years later my mother explained the reason for the garden visits. Mom told me that Aunt Jean had once lured her sweetly to a sunroom off the main hospital hallway. My mom had moved just out of sight of the other patients and visitors when Aunt Jean lunged at her and tried to attack her. Mom said she was somehow able to jump free before the attack turned violent. My mother never again visited Aunt Jean within the walls of the state hospital. I guess that's why those outdoor garden visits always felt so strange. There was a blanket of fear when we visited Aunt Jean. The conversations were not like normal ones between two people, and I was always glad when Aunt Jean left the garden and headed back to the hospital and we headed back to the car. But sometimes, Aunt Jean got in the car with us. That is what happened that day as we drove down the city streets.

Grandma and Mom sat in the front seat. Aunt Jean and I sat together in the back seat. Her hair was messy and unkempt. She had glaringly bright red lipstick on. She had on a big flowery dress, white short socks with slip-on penny loafers, and unshaved legs. She wore Rosaries around her neck, and she repeated everything my grandma said. I was an average-size child of probably forty pounds. Aunt Jean was at least two hundred pounds. I worried she could grab me in the back seat while we drove in traffic. I knew I would die before anyone could even stop the car. I probably stared more than normal children would, but I didn't want to take my eyes off of her. Quite literally, Aunt Jean terrified me.

She looked crazy and acted crazy. I felt great relief when she was out of the car after those doctor visits and we dropped her off at the hospital. I knew better than to ask questions, voice my fear, or even address Aunt Jean's strange behavior and appearance. It was not to be spoken about, and I knew the price would be a beating if I did. Eventually the rides with Aunt Jean became less and less frequent. Later in my life, she would be at Grandma's house sitting in the big chair with her crazy hair, bold lipstick, and odd, halting speech, smoking one cigarette after another. I always said hi and hightailed it out of the house. I would run so I wouldn't be trapped—like I was in the car. As I got older, I never wanted to attack anyone like Aunt Jean did. This gave me some solace that I wasn't crazy like she was, even though I sometimes felt confused by my unexplained fear and panic.

Years later, Aunt Jean died from obesity and smoking that led to a heart attack. I heard many more stories of her childhood, my grandfather's dislike for her early in life, and her eventual journey into insanity. Did she have multiple personality disorder? Was she schizophrenic? Was she brain damaged from falling on her head as a toddler from a second-floor apartment? Stories were revealed. Answers were never clear. I wasn't sad when I heard that she had died. I didn't see anyone shed a tear. There was no service. She was just buried. No one really spoke much about her again.

I'm Not a Spoiled Mama's Girl

I started kindergarten. For my fifth birthday in the summer that year, I got a raincoat and matching plaid umbrella. That day, as I modeled my new outfit and twirled my umbrella, I felt like the richest, most special little girl on the block. I could not wait for the cooler weather and rain so that I could be the most stylish kindergartner in class. I had lost my two front teeth months before by running headfirst into a playmate. I don't know who cried the hardest, him or me, but I could truly wish for a pretty smile as my parents continuously sang, "All I want for Christmas is my two front teeth." Fall rolled around quickly, and with new teeth buds in my smile, I started my first day of school. I did fine, and when school let out, I proceeded to the car like all the other kids. When Mom asked what we did, I told her about my day. She asked what we would do the next day, and I didn't know. I really didn't know. I panicked—real, truly painful, paralyzing panic. I began to cry and announced I didn't want to go back to school again. I didn't understand my fear. I could not explain it. I was too young, but what I came to realize was that if, as my mother preached, "The world is a big evil place, so stay close to your family because they're all you can count on," then I was in trouble. My unconscious knew I lived a dual life of unpredictable cruelty, abuse, and insanity along with normal days of family events with chores, play, meals, and what appeared to be normal everyday activity. So my kindergarten life became a torturous daily ordeal of living for the predictable family on weekends. I cried, vomited, shook, and even ran away from the classroom one day with the teacher on my heels. Mom screamed, yelled, and spanked me. She dragged me to the car and threatened to take me to Aunt Jean's psychiatrist just to scare me. I cried and begged her not to, but the terror, vomiting, and crying continued. It was a heartbreaking tragedy that I remember so vividly now. It was as terrifying and confusing to me as the rest of my life when things did not make sense. I did not understand why I cried when my schoolmates didn't. My kindergarten teacher was old and tall and smelled funny. She declared that I was a spoiled mama's girl. It was another missed opportunity to spot abuse, and to add insult to injury, she humiliated me and I owned the humiliation. Oh, how I could have helped a little Janey. I would have intervened if I were the teacher. I would have called for help.

If I hadn't been so traumatized, I might have been embarrassed. But I was trying to live through the terror of the day while experiencing a black hole of confusion. What scared me so much? I went to school. I cried. Some weeks when abuses occurred at home and intrinsic memories flooded the memory box in my head, the panic and crying were even worse. Since I never remembered the sexual abuse of my father in my bed, my brother abusing me physically and sexually, or both of them hurting me, the increased anxiety and fear had no context. I felt damaged, broken. I was blonde and sweet and had big green eyes, and I was from a good Catholic family who went to Mass every Sunday. What could possibly scare me so? I called the horrible anxiety a "funny feeling." There was nothing funny about it. I was a terribly tortured child. I somehow lived through the constant overriding terror of that chaotic year, week after week of torture. How did I learn? I have no idea. The pattern of abuse, forgetting, fearing the big, evil world, feeling crazy with anxiety, trying to make sense of a "funny feeling," and panic with no known cause continued for the next several years of my life.

If the world was a big, evil place and I needed to stay close to my family, what hope did I have outside the home? I had already suffered so much abuse from my family, how would I possibly survive in the big, evil world? To a child, the world is anything outside his or her family. For me, the world was school, starting with kindergarten and the tall teacher who had a strange smell. Each teacher every year could be more evil than the last. Every new, unfamiliar experience did not cause normal anticipation. My life was at stake! Each new school year, a new high school job, a new public high school, trying to make friends, and even the beginning of nursing school created panic. No one knew how miserable I was, but I was terrified, and I learned to hide it so well. Eventually, when I moved to my nursing dorm and wonderful friendships developed and I started to have fun on dates and at parties with friends, the terror of the so-called big, evil world began to fade. Being out of my house of horrors, I found myself and a newfound confidence. My mother repeated that mantra even after I had moved from our hometown, but it finally had lost its power. What a cruel thing to say to a child. What a sad and crazy belief used to control her kids and prevent them from leaving the nest. It eventually pushed me further from the evil of the family and closer to the goodness of the world.

PROFOUNDLY QUIET

It all happened so fast. One day my family returned from a Sunday Mass, and the phone rang. I could tell from my mother's voice that she was very excited. When she hung up, she said that my grandmother told her that the house across the street from her was for sale. I didn't know we were even thinking about moving. In fact, I didn't completely understand what moving was. This was the only house I had ever known. All seven of us piled into the family car and drove the fifteen minutes to a house across the street from my grandparents' house. It was a white frame house with an attached garage and a well-manicured yard with big trees. Within a month from when we first looked at this house, my parents sold the house we were living in. I had to leave everything I ever knew behind.

This new house was a nice house. It was bigger than our other house. It had an extra family room and carpet in the living room, which I thought only rich people had. One major difference screamed out to me. It was profoundly quiet. There were at least four to five kids in every house in my old neighborhood. From dawn until dusk, children's voices of all ages could always be heard—yelling, laughing, screaming, and playing. But this new house was in a neighborhood where people's kids had already grown up, and the quiet was deafening. It felt foreign and unsettling, but my parents seemed so happy to be settled in our new home. I will admit that at first it was fun to have my grandparents across the street. It was also within walking distance to school. The best part was where I slept. At six years old, I was finally old enough to sleep in the top bunk, and that changed everything about my bedroom.

The smaller space of the top bunk, filled with pillows and stuffed animals, created a sweet haven that was comfy and warm. While stuffed animals, dolls, and pillows created a safe sanctuary, my real security was the wooden ladder. My sisters slept across from each other: one in a twin bed and the other in the bottom bunk. It made more sense with different school start times. I knew at least one of them would wake if a stalker clambered up to the top bunk, and there was precious little space for groping hands and unwanted lips to violate my innocence. I drifted off more quickly and slept more deeply in the refuge of my lofty oasis.

The top bunk was wonderful, but once I descended the ladder, I was no longer really safe. Unconsciously, I was always on heightened alert. I was acutely vigilant of shadows or suspicious movement, keenly alert to the slightest creaks in the floor from menacing footsteps, and intensely sensitive to musky cigarette and perspiration warning of impending danger. All of my senses were amplified, and my limbic system was in overdrive. I had never lived any other way. This was my normal, and this house became my home for over ten years as I struggled through the incongruities of my life. Intermittent bouts of anxiety were interspersed with warm-weather kickball and careening down the sledding hills after a major winter storm. Hidden depression was countered by making new friends and the pride of being labeled the best third baseman on our softball team. I always felt different from my friends at school and the neighborhood kids, but I was becoming incredibly adept at hiding spells of anxiety and terror that could rise like a monster from the sea. I never knew when a peaceful sail in a gentle sea would suddenly explode into an explosive tidal wave tossing me into the jagged, rocky shore. Worse than not knowing when the tide would turn was my inability to comprehend why. Part of me knew why. I just wouldn't get a glimpse of that why until I was old enough and brave enough to sail directly into the storm to reach the safety of the warm, sandy shore.

A Most Perfect Day at School

New home or not, school continued to be a struggle. The panic was greater on some days than on others. Of course, I couldn't remember the horrible traumas inflicted the nights before, but that did not lessen the waves of panic. My mother labeled me the "spoiled, nervous child." I often started school terrified and with tears in my eyes, but I knew I had no choice but to go. I actually liked some of the kids and made a couple of friends, but it was drilled into me that the world was a big, evil place, and I was told those friends would never be there for me. How could I win? I managed to get through the agonizing months of first grade, the day-after-day terror, until Christmas. All the other kids were full of excitement for Christmas to come. And I couldn't wait because I knew it would be a break from my daily fear and anxiety.

On the last day before Christmas break, we returned, single file, to our classroom after recess, to find red net stockings filled with fruit and candy on our desk. I was SO excited. We were told that St. Nicholas must have come while we were out of the room. We were then led single file into the cafeteria, where we always ate our bagged lunches. The smell of hamburgers filled the cafeteria. I was so confused because the pastor of the church connected to the school never let anyone use the beautiful stainless steel kitchen. He didn't want anybody to dull the shine or dirty the pots and pans. But that day was different.

It was exciting to see mothers bustling through the kitchen as they prepared hamburger lunches for all the kids. All eight grades were in the cafeteria at the same time. It was against the rules to talk at lunch. We had typically been directed to eat in strict silence, so being able to not only sit next to your friend but also be able to talk with her was an amazing and exciting surprise. The oppressive rules in the cafeteria were gone, and chatter and laughter filled the air. We all lined up and got a hamburger on a bun, chips, and even a chocolate chip cookie! My joy and my anxiety were extremely confusing. But for that moment, that day at lunch, I was actually happy because this was such a special treat.

This had absolutely been the most perfect time at school in my two years of angst. In the midst of laughter and joy, I heard the familiar sound of the transport cart used to transport books and supplies. The next thing I saw was the third-grade teacher rolling into the cafeteria with a reel-to-reel movie projector and a large, thin, round silver canister. We watched in anticipation as she threaded the movie into the machine and a bright light clicked on. Suddenly the Disney movie *Dumbo* began to play on a large white screen. This was not only magical because of the food, fun, and movie, but it made up the only two hours I had ever spent at school without severe anxiety. For the first time, I became just one of the other excited kids—so surprised by all the festivities in anticipation of Christmas. Every time I smell hamburgers, every time I see a picture of an elephant, every Christmas, I remember that special day where the world was not a big, evil place and when I shared the joy of friendship and fun without fear. As I grew older, I experienced more days at school without anxiety. I knew the panic could strike as unexpectedly as lightning, but there were never any storm clouds to warn me. Without any extrinsic memory of what had happened, I fell victim to this unpredictable darkness, aware that just like a bolt of lightning, I could be struck at any time.

My Fair Lady

In grade school, none of my friends suspected that there was anything different about me. I became a master at masking my feelings. I had a couple of close girlfriends by second and third grade, but that threesome ended when one moved away. Her parents built a house in another part of the city. Patty and I were then left to be best friends, and we often played after school or did homework together at her house, never mine. I was amazed by how calm her mother was and by how no one in her home seemed afraid. There was much laughter. One spring afternoon her mother called my mom and asked her if I could join Patty for a special live showing of *My Fair Lady* at the local playhouse. I had no idea what *My Fair Lady* was, but it was a school night, and

I was thrilled when Mom said yes. I counted off the days of the calendar for two weeks with anticipation of the special treat of going to a theater on a school night. I had never seen a musical before—and I could not wait to see what it was! Patty fell asleep in her theater chair for part of the play. And while I didn't dare, I wanted to wake her because she was missing a really fun performance. I was hooked on musicals, never having known that you could enjoy a story with singing. I got home late, around 10:00 p.m., and went straight to bed. I already had a note in my backpack for my third-grade teacher because I was going to sleep in an extra hour the next morning and miss morning Mass before school started. It seemed like a fairy-tale evening. But when I awoke, the other kids were out of the house. Dad had left for work, and Mom was standing next to my bed in her housecoat with the strangest look on her face. I felt a sudden shiver of terror through my body. She pulled the covers back, pulled down my panties, and started to lick between my legs. I was terrified. It was as if my mom was not in her own body. It didn't last long because I started to move and struggle to get out of the bed. Mom stood upright and said, "Don't tell me you didn't like that." She unsnapped her robe, exposing her wrinkled body and droopy breasts. I was horrified. She then walked out of the room and I was frozen. I got up, got dressed, left to walk to school with an incredible sense of fear and anxiety. Tears rolled from my eyes on my walk to school. It was horrible because I didn't know why I was crying. I didn't know what caused such terror. Somehow my magical night was ruined, and I felt crazy. As always, I masked the feelings, somehow sucked in the tears, and kept my gaze down to the floor. I was exhausted when I got home from school that day. I thought it was just my late night at *My Fair Lady*. I love musicals, but I never watched *My Fair Lady* on TV with the family and refused to go see it at the local outdoor opera in town.

MEMORIES SNEAKING THROUGH

When I was in third and fourth grade, a strange occurrence would happen every night as I began to fall asleep. Just as I began to slip into a twilight sleep, I would have a terrifying image and visceral experience. I would feel an intense pressure on my face and mouth. I could feel hair, my mouth felt full, and my face was soaked. It happened regularly, and every time I bolted upright, gagging and panicked. Night after night after night I would be jarred awake in terror. Trying to catch my breath, I would realize that the gagging and smothering were just part of a dream. Finally, exhausted, I would drift off. But I began to dread closing my eyes as I fought to stay awake to avoid the horror.

One day while playing with my friends, I found out how babies were born. I was shocked, but suddenly I thought maybe I wasn't crazy after all. Several more months passed with the same nightly experience. I mustered the courage to ask Mom if I could be remembering my birth. I told her everything I felt, everything I saw, with every sensation. I explained logically to her that I must be reliving my birth.

She told me that was impossible, and I should never speak of it again. Now, I not only had to go to bed at night and still experience the same horrible sensations—gagging and fear—but after our talk I felt shame because I couldn't stop it. I just accepted that I must have something wrong with my brain, so I added a prayer when I got under the covers. I prayed I would not grow up to be like Aunt Jean. I was desperate to stop the nightly torture. My girlfriend had a bedroom that was painted pink, and the ceiling was wallpapered with dark pink roses. She told me that on nights when she couldn't fall asleep, she counted the roses. That is exactly what I started to do. I closed my eyes, I saw her ceiling, and I started counting. No matter what I started to sense or see, I forced myself, even if I had to whisper out loud, to count the number of roses that were on my friend's ceiling. My nightly revulsion finally started to fade back into the box of explicit memories, but it was the closest I ever came to remembering any of my abuse during my childhood.

While I always had implicit memories, and that nightly occurrence was definitely an implicit memory, the explicit memories would stay sealed in a black box in the deepest recesses of my mind. Like the lock on a chest corroding under the weight of the sea, the lock on my hidden box of memories ultimately disintegrated from years of repression. Floating to the surface, my memories were revealed by the light, and my childhood was exposed as a horrific story of survival.

Unconditional Love

I always wanted a dog. I begged and promised I would take care of it. But Mom said she didn't want a dog because they were dirty, and she said we would never get one. From a very young age I loved animals, especially dogs, and they seemed to love me too. Just holding or petting a friend's dog seemed to calm me. I knew dogs didn't judge me for my feelings of despair and anxiety. They didn't label me as nervous or crazy. They just wagged their tails, loved my affection, and licked me when I approached. Dogs accepted me with no judgment, which was more than I could expect from many humans. One night a miracle happened.

I was in the family room watching TV after dinner when I heard some commotion and crying at the front door. As I got up to see what was going on, I saw Mom standing with a stunned look on her face, holding a black, furry puppy in her arms. She had taken a part-time job at a dental office. I later learned that the adult daughter of one of her coworkers had gotten a new puppy but couldn't keep it because her apartment didn't allow dogs. Somehow in conversation at work that day, my mom's coworker thought Mom had expressed interest in adopting the puppy. Without warning, Mom was holding a ten-week-old puppy. The original owner provided a dog bed, dog food, and a lot of her tears on this curly, black ball of fluff as she handed over this adorable puppy to our family. Just as suddenly as the original owner appeared, she abruptly left, crying all the way to her car.

I was ecstatic! Mom was shocked. But she couldn't help but be as amused as we kids were at this incredible little black ball of fun and fluff. We were told not to get too attached because we might not keep her. But since the holidays were coming, my grandmother named the dog Holly for the season of Christmas. And before we knew it, Holly was there to stay. She became an official part of the family.

We all fell in love with Holly, and all took care of her. I was comforted by her company as we went for walks and visited my grandmother. Holly often slept on the couch with me while I was watching TV, and she even helped me with my homework. It was the beginning of my love affair with animals, learning of their unconditional love and acceptance. Even when I felt a little less normal, I could count on

Holly being by my side. A constant source of comfort during my dark days, Holly was an entertainer who delighted in making me laugh with her silly, playful antics, gentle wagging tail, and warm snuggles and joyful doggy kisses. Holly grew to be my best friend and my greatest comfort, and I shielded her during tumultuous fights or when angry Mom came home. We took care of each other. I always knew she was a gift from heaven.

That spring Holly witnessed my abuse. She and I walked in the backyard, where Anthony was digging a hole for a tree that Mom wanted planted. I didn't say much and just walked over to watch. Anthony shot me a glance of disgust. I suppose my existence annoyed him. Anthony stopped digging long enough to take a drink from the cup on the ground just a few feet away. I bent over to see how deep the hole was. In an instant, I felt the shovel slam down on my back. The pain was excruciating. I fell into the hole and could not catch my breath. Anthony walked away and into the house as if I didn't exist. Holly stood by the hole, watching me climb out. I was crying in pain, and she was there to lick my tears. I could only crawl for a few feet. My back was throbbing. After a couple of minutes, I was eventually able to stand. Holly stayed by my side the whole time. It probably took me ten minutes to get to my bedroom. I lay in my bed, on my side with my knees bent. I fell asleep despite the throbbing pain. When I woke up, I realized Holly had nestled herself on the bed behind the bend of my knees. I knew I had gotten hurt but couldn't remember exactly how. There would be many more times that I would have back spasms. What eight-year-old girl has such a painful injury with no known cause? Mom thought I was faking it, so I learned not to complain. The side-lying position, with a heating pad to warm my back, seemed to decrease the pain and relieve muscle spasms. For years I thought I must have fallen outside and injured myself. Almost fifteen years later, I would have a laminectomy to remove the disc between my L4 and L5 vertebrae, exactly where the shovel slammed down on my spine. Holly saw what happened. Her gentle support and company were a sweet comfort to a little girl. It was years later that I finally remembered the senseless cruelty that Holly witnessed.

Yellow Tulips

When you're little, everyone asks what your favorite color is. I always knew mine was yellow, but I never explained why. Every year after a long, cold winter, we all looked forward to beautiful spring weather. We were the second owners of the house we lived in, and the previous owner had planted tulip bulbs on the side of the house. Every spring I visited the tulips as they emerged from the dark, cold ground. Even as a young girl, it struck me how these tulips could live deep in cold darkness all winter and then emerge so triumphantly every spring. Every morning before school, I quietly walked to the side of the house to visit them. First there would just be a tiny touch of green breaking through the hard clay. Every day, inch by inch, they started to rise up out of the ground. They eventually became tight, green buds, and as the weather got warmer and the days grew longer, those green buds opened up into the most beautiful yellow tulips. No one else in the family seemed to care about the tulips and how beautiful they were, but I did. I understood the flowers. Just as the tulips had survived another long, dark, cold winter buried by dirt, I felt like I had survived another year of darkness, buried by stress and confusion. The yellow tulips were mine. They seemed discarded by the family. I wasn't sure why, but I understood that feeling. No one cared for or tended to them, and yet they still emerged every year. I pulled the weeds away from them. I touched them gently. I told them they were beautiful. I knew how they felt. I didn't want them to feel neglected, ignored, uncared for, or unloved. I saw their beauty. I saw the vibrant yellow in their petals and the deep green in their strong stems. I recognized that they were delicate and strong at the same time. And I loved them. Yellow is still my favorite color. Tulips are still my favorite flower. And after almost fifty years, I still wonder about them at that house. Every spring, if the house still stands as it did when I was a child, I know that they will emerge. They will have survived the cold darkness of another winter. I hope someone loves them and sees their beauty as much as I did.

GRANDMA'S HOUSE IS EMPTY

For a couple of years I got a reprieve from the anxiety. I wasn't sure why, but it may have had something to do with Anthony leaving for college. He was out of state and no longer a daily threat, so I found some peace. His constant taunts and cruel teasing brought some calmness to our home and to my spirit. Even though Dad was still there and often waiting, at least half of the adult men were gone. At that same time, my parents were consumed with the fact that my grandmother had been diagnosed with breast cancer. I focused on friends and softball and school projects. At ten years old, I felt gangly and clumsy, caught in between being a child and a young woman. I had no idea how sick my grandmother was, so it was a surprise to learn of an emergency concerning either of my grandparents after the phone rang one spring Sunday afternoon. My parents ran across the street to my grandparents' house, but this emergency was for my grandfather, who was suffering severe chest pain. I watched with fear as an ambulance came and picked him up. It was then that I noticed how frail and weak my grandmother looked trying to walk to the car to head to the hospital. She had always been an overweight, square woman. But I could see in the sunlight that her pale skin seemed to hang from her frame.

Seeing my grandfather being transported down the road with my parents driving behind the ambulance and my grandmother in the back seat suddenly made it very clear that they were old. It's odd how I never noticed it before. I found out late that evening that my grandfather did, in fact, have a heart attack. Two days later, while he was in the hospital, he had another massive heart attack and died. Within four months after his death, the cancer took my grandmother. We were back at the same funeral home, having lost both grandparents within a few months. Everything had become a blur of funeral home, crying adults, extended family, caskets, and scary dead bodies.

In the months after their deaths, I tried to steer clear of my crying mother and my angry, irritable father. While I don't think Dad had the ability to truly love, I think he liked the support my grandparents had provided. Since he never had a real family of his own, this was as close as it got.

Over the next several months, they cleaned out my grandparents' house, including the garage, which was filled with truckloads of wood that my grandfather had collected as a carpenter of thirty years.

Since the adults were grieving and adjusting to the major loss in their lives, I enjoyed the peace. It was quiet, and I stayed in the shadows as Mom, Dad, and Mom's sisters settled my grandparents' affairs. Most kids crave attention. I loved the lack of it. I wondered why that felt so safe and comforting. While I couldn't identify any reason for the tranquility, I just accepted and enjoyed it.

Within the year, my mom's oldest sister had moved her family into my grandparents' house, and life seemed to settle down. Calm was never permanent in my family, so just as life settled, more major change was looming in the not-too-distant future. The familiar family chaos would soon return.

I SMILED AND WAVED GOODBYE

Anthony had gone away to college in Denver and then in Kansas City on scholarships. It was easier with him gone. While I didn't understand the complete reason why life was less stressful with him away, I certainly felt a horrible sense of dread when he came back to our hometown to complete college at a university close to home. Fortunately, shortly after he moved back home, he met a girl. It was obvious that they were serious. They went to classes together, they studied together, they went out, and somehow my life got easier. His temper wasn't as bad because he was focused on his girlfriend, and he loved the attention she gave him. I thought his girlfriend was beautiful. She had very dark brown hair and beautiful white skin. I tried to tell myself that she was nice to me because she somehow liked me, but she really only tolerated me. It didn't really matter; things were better than what it was like before she was in his life. They dated for a couple of years and got engaged. She seemed to fit in as much as you could in our family, and our dog, Holly, loved her, so that made her OK in my book.

Their wedding was very small and in a Catholic church, not because they had any sense of faith but because my parents and her parents insisted that was where they needed to marry. I wore a simple blue dress with a stripe of flowers down the front of it. My face was broken out, I was gangly, and I wondered if I would ever be as pretty and sophisticated as my brother's new wife. After a simple reception, the newlyweds waved as they walked out the door. I felt very, very happy. I tried to convince myself that my joy was for them, but that wasn't really true. I didn't care if I ever saw him again. I felt terrible and guilty about that thought. I never shared it with anyone. Regardless of whether I was sinning or not in the context of being a good Catholic girl, I couldn't shake that feeling. His absence lightened my life, and I was glad he was no longer around. The mothers of the newlyweds cried as their married children drove away. I didn't. I smiled and waved goodbye with a great sense of relief.

REBELLION EVERYWHERE

The wedding was barely over when everything started to crumble out of control. I don't know why I thought my life would ever be calm or my family would function without fighting, because that was a fairytale. My life never settled down. There was always chaos, strife, and tension. I was growing up in the sixties and seventies. Hippies, drugs, the sexual revolution, Vietnam, and rock 'n' roll were in the news and in my life. My sisters got jobs while they started classes at a local college. Mike grew his hair long and fought constantly with my parents. More than his hair changed. He started hanging out with the kids at our school who did drugs. He criticized me constantly for not being one of the sexy, popular girls and not partying and drinking like the cool kids at his high school. When our parents weren't home, he blasted his rock music so loud that the dishes in the china cabinet shook. If I tried to turn the stereo volume down, Mike physically slammed me across the room. I was so miserable. To make matters even worse, the house I knew best growing up was on the market because the color of our neighborhood was changing.

I didn't understand anything. I didn't really understand hippies or drugs or Vietnam or racism. And I knew I should not ask about subjects like these because there was always so much screaming, fighting, and even angry holes punched in walls. Before I knew it, we were moving out of the house. We lived in a rental home close to my school until my parents could figure out where we would settle. Mike was constantly stoned and was growing pot in the backyard of the rental house behind some old tools. He showed me his stash in a small locked box in his closet and then threatened to kill me if I told our parents.

Not only did I feel crazy but also now everything about my life was crazy. My parents soon found the marijuana and confronted Mike, who reacted in rage and then withdrew in a haze of pot smoke.

My sisters, Jenny and Debbie, who had both been dating guys my parents did not approve of, moved out of the house while we were all at work and school, leaving a note saying that since they had discussed moving into an apartment on their own and had been accused of being whores, they felt this was the only way that they could successfully move away. I felt alone and trapped and spent most nights in my bedroom crying myself to sleep.

I didn't understand what was wrong with people of color. I didn't really understand what had happened in Vietnam. I hated my brother's pot-smoking friends, and my sisters had abandoned me. I was completely and utterly alone. I continued to go to school, and as I had done all my life, I wiped away the tears and lived with incredible anxiety and fear. I was becoming a master of acting like nothing was wrong in my life as I survived one day at a time.

The secrets were piling up, and I felt as if I had no place to turn for help. The reality was, I didn't.

I Liked That Dress Before

I was floating in a sea of crazy family chaos while still trying to join in school functions with the group of girls I called friends. My group of friends were in the middle. We weren't totally unpopular and backwards, but we weren't the popular cheerleaders or druggies either. I desperately wanted to be like my friends, and I was terrified they would learn I wasn't. I already felt so isolated at home, I didn't want to lose this group of friends. I never confided in anyone about how I felt or how my mom cried all the time about my druggie brother and sisters she labeled whores. In fact, I did just the opposite. I became so skilled at creating a facade, I really don't think any of my friends suspected I was suffering in any way. We were sharing our makeup and cutting our hair like Farrah

Fawcett. Tight bell-bottoms, long beads, and flowing hair made us feel older. At thirteen, I was one of the last girls to start my period. I thought starting my period would somehow force my family to view me as a young woman, not a child. The monthly, scarlet stain gave me a false sense that growing up would afford me more respect. I was wrong.

One of my first school dances was coming up. I got my first pair of wedge heels and a soft knit cream dress. My blonde hair was long, to the middle of my back, and I was starting to develop a shape. I loved that dress with a soft silk bow that tied in the back to accentuate my developing curves.

One day I came home from school. As I walked in the door, I froze. My mother was at work, and no one else should have been at home. But my father was. Something was not right. I should have left the house and stayed outside. I should have run. I should have done anything, but I didn't. I just froze, and later I blamed myself. I took a deep breath as if nothing was wrong and went into my bedroom. I called out from my room and asked my dad why he was home. My pretty dress had been laid out on my bed. Dad pointed to the dress and told me to put it on. I was scared not to obey, but also embarrassed and terrified because he would not leave the room. I kept my back to him as I undressed, but he came up behind me rubbing his body up against my back while he rubbed his hands across my small breasts. I could feel myself leaving my body, going numb, and seeing the juniper trees outside my window. I watched from a dissociated distance as he pushed me down on the bed, and I choked and gagged as he forced himself on me and had oral sex. Watching from the junipers outside my window, I saw him stand as he zipped up his pants and look at me with a sickening smirk. Before he walked out the door, he said, "Clean yourself up and don't you ever tell anyone, or I'll do the same thing to your kids someday and then kill you all." Oh, this sounded familiar. I had never had a chance to put on the dress like he had ordered. I felt dirty, ashamed, and stupid for not leaving the house when I had the chance. But those thoughts floated away.

I got off the bed, changed into my after-school clothes, went into the bathroom, washed my face and rinsed out my mouth, wondering why I was so shaky and why I felt so sick to my stomach. My face was blotchy from crying, but I didn't know why I had been crying. As I went back in my bedroom, I put my dress on a hanger in my closet. I had liked that dress before, but for some reason nowI hated it. I kicked my heels under the bed. I pulled my books out to study for a test the next day.

As I sat on the floor in my room studying, my mind drifted to thoughts of the dance on Saturday. I wondered why I was no longer excited to wear my new outfit and go with my friends. But as usual, I felt just a little bit off and extremely anxious for no reason. What was wrong with me? I felt helpless; I simply couldn't make any sense out of my random moods.

I Could Smile Again

I drove with my parents every week to look for houses where only white people lived. I had really only known one area of the city, one school. But I was so depressed that I said I liked the house that they chose to build, forty-five minutes south of where we had lived all our lives.

We moved, and I started my education at a public school for the first time in my life. I was terrified. I knew no one, no one wore uniforms, it was much less rigid, and no one reached out to be my friend. All the cliques had already formed. I struggled through the days at school, speaking to no one, having no friends to laugh with, no one to sit with at lunch. But it didn't really matter because I was so scared and so depressed that I couldn't eat. I lost ten pounds and my clothes hung on me. There were no neighbors yet because the subdivision was brand new. We could have just as well moved to another planet because that's how strange and foreign everything was. I would occasionally call friends from my old neighborhood. One of my old friends told me a family friend of theirs had moved into the same area where I then lived and probably went to my new school. She gave me her name, and I was desperate for anything familiar. Even in the midst of my depression, I picked up the phone, called information, and found her number. Her name was Lindsey. And my world was going to change. I found hope.

We met at Lindsey's house. She was a connection to the old and a bridge to the present. Her family was bustling and happy, and I felt joy for the first time in months. Lindsey and I became best friends. Even though she was a year younger, we would meet before class, and I had someone to sit with at lunch. The desperate school year ended, but I had a friend and a connection to a healthy, normal family that gave me faith. I could smile again. We spent hours on the phone, summer days at the pool, and many hours listening to albums, reading *Seventeen* magazine, and talking about boys. We laughed. We were girls. I had a life again, and I loved being with her family and spent as much time as I could at her home.

I Said No

With my sisters gone, I slept on a full bed, and the room was all mine. There were nights my father was in my room, in my bed, fondling me. As I had always done, I froze and dissociated and forgot by the morning although the anxiety was high, and I felt off for days. After each abuse, I floated into my yellow curtains hanging on my window and watched from a distance. I hated him. I hated his fingers; I hated his smell; I hated his skin. I hated every part of him. After he was done, I would roll up in a ball and try hard not to feel dirty and meaningless. Over the years I developed a chant: I softly repeated, "I don't want to be here anymore; I don't want to be here anymore; I don't want to be here anymore." I whispered the mantra over and over and over until

I fell asleep. It became my escape. But then I would see him the next morning and fall into a state of panic. I experienced such frustration and confusion because I had no idea why I felt such intense, unexplainable feelings.

One evening after I had been to Lindsey's house, I felt happy and light. I had enjoyed such a good time with Lindsey sharing the dreams and hopes of a seventeen-year-old entering young adulthood. I had just turned out the lights and was drifting off to sleep when suddenly I realized my father was in the room and trying to climb on top of me. He had no underwear on, and I instantly remembered what he wanted. But this time, instead of freezing, instead of watching from a distance, I felt stronger. I knocked him off of me, stood up and said *no*! As I ran toward the door to leave my room, I grabbed a marker that I had on the calendar on my door and threw it at him. In that split second, I saw him fumbling to get his balance and stand up. He looked so old, ugly, and stupid. And then I ran. I ran into the bathroom, shut the door behind me and locked it. I slid down the wall into a huddle, holding my knees close to my chest, and I started praying over and over, "Help me, God; help me, God; help me, God." I waited for pounding on the door. I waited for the little key to open it. I cried and trembled in terror as I waited and continued to whisper, "Help me, God." Seconds felt like hours, and the minutes felt like days. There was no pounding at the door. The lock did not move. And what was probably only fifteen minutes felt like a lifetime. With shaking legs, I pushed myself up the wall and moved closer to the bathroom door. I couldn't remember why I was so terrified. I held my ear against the door, knowing that there must have been something dangerous out there and maybe I would hear some sound and would remember why I was so terrified. After another ten minutes, my heart pounding in my chest, I got up the nerve to unlock the bathroom door and open it. There was no one in the hall. There was no one in my bedroom. I slid under the covers. I thought that I must have been walking in my sleep and had a very bad dream. In the midst of the fear, a feeling of victory swept over me. It felt like I had won a game or aced a test, but it was something even stronger and sweeter. What a strange and wonderful feeling. I was exhausted and fell asleep. I woke up the next morning and picked up the marker that had somehow landed on the other side of the room. I wasn't hungry for breakfast. I got ready for school and looked forward to the next time Lindsey and I would listen to records in her room and sing along to our favorite tunes, laughing and talking as young women do.

I Did It Anyway

In the 1960s and 1970s many girls chose to become nurses or teachers. I loved science, and despite my abuse, I somehow did exceptionally well in school. I decided I wanted to go to nursing school. Mom could not imagine being a nurse, so she tried to talk me out of it. Her narcissism was showing. If she couldn't feel it, then no one could. But I loved the thought of helping people and knowing all the science involved in nursing.

I applied and was accepted to a nursing program at a local junior college affiliated with a large teaching hospital. I started to plan for the fall, when I would begin my classes and clinicals. Because of the rigorous schedule, the school suggested I move into the dorm. When Mom heard that, she exploded. She told me there was no reason I should move out of our home, and only sluts lived outside of their parents' home before they got married. When she was raging, there was little anyone could do to stop her. I spoke of it no more and convinced myself that everything would work out fine.

But it didn't. Nursing school students were low on the totem pole. When we were assigned a patient, we were to create a care plan and write note cards for every medication that patient was taking. Being the lowest on the totem pole meant that we were behind physicians, the residents, the interns, the physical therapists, and then the med students. Rarely could we get access to the patient's chart until 8:00 p.m. or 9 p.m. Preparing for the clinical the next day for any one patient could take up to four hours. Between classes and clinicals, I was exhausted.

I was living on three to four hours of sleep and was living with that same underlying panic—making my way in the big, evil world. The final straw came in November, when a late-autumn storm blew in with sleet and snow. I was up until 1:00 a.m. preparing for my patient and left the house at 4:30 a.m., before snowplows even began to clear the roads. I drove the forty-minute drive, which took me well over two hours. The roads were slick with ice underneath the snow, and I could barely see as I drove to my clinical preparation with my instructor and my fellow students. Mom and Dad didn't care if I was safe, if school was intensely grueling, or if I was exhausted. They would not hear of me moving into the dorm.

The next semester, I started working as a nurse's aide every other weekend in addition to meeting my demanding school schedule. I was able to make enough money to pay a monthly fee to live in the dorm connected to the hospital. I could work with my fellow nursing students to continue a maddening schedule. I enlisted the help of my friend Lindsey. I bought cheap sheets and a bedspread on clearance, and she helped me move in. Mom refused to talk to me, and as usual, Dad followed her lead. I walked in and out of the house with arms full of books and clothes, passing both parents, who looked past me as if I didn't exist. Neither of them would speak to me for three weeks. But I was there. I was safe. The support and extra sleep allowed me to function.

After the first month, the silence at home began to lift because we nursing students often went home on weekends. Whenever I went home, I usually arrived on Friday around 2:00 p.m. That gave me enough time to clean the entire house. I mopped, swept, dusted, cleaned bathrooms, and folded clothes until 5:00 p.m. As the silence started to lift, the fact that I lived at the dorm became less of an issue as long as I did the weekly chores. I sometimes only had a dollar in my pocket to last me a week. But I didn't care. I was completely committed to school and began to make friends. As students, we were a team. We shared drug note cards, exchanged information on shared patients, and cried and laughed through the intensity of all that was required.

Nursing students at that time helped run the hospitals. I had my constant balancing act of keeping Mom appeased by being her personal maid and keeping up my grades. I didn't know it then, but my career would allow me to set myself free for a life in which I could support myself and leave the madness behind.

It Was a Magical Time

While it would seem impossible that we were able to find any time for outside activities, we nurses learned to live on little sleep. I had started to blossom in my femininity and my confidence. I started to meet pharmacy students, physical therapy students, and other young men. I loved the attention! I loved the good touch! I loved the laughter and meeting their families. Somehow, dating made me feel normal.

Sometimes I dated two and even three boys at a time. There was no sexual activity beyond kissing and light petting because we were all good Catholic girls and were going to wait until we got married. Occasionally one boy would touch my heart more than others. But ultimately, as with most matters of young love, the relationships were short-lived. I found solace in my friends through the breakups and would continue to date again. Dating was actually more than just emotional—it was also financial. Unlike most of the other girls, whose moms took them shopping or whose parents paid for their education, I received no help. Back then, boys paid for the dates. I got to go out to eat, go to ball games, and attend movies. I was free from my family and felt cared for in a normal way. For the few years that it lasted, living in the dorm with friends and dating was the happiest, most carefree period of my life. I still reminisce about those college years, and my heart is thankful. I don't so much remember the tough courses or the grueling schedule, but I fondly recall the jokes and laughter and shared lives that we all experienced in that old brick building connected to the hospital. It was a magical time.

FINDING MY WAY

The magical period of living in the dorms with other nursing students, working hard, and enjoying deep friendships inevitably ended. I was one of the youngest in my class, and at only twenty years old, I graduated from nursing school, passed my state boards, and became an RN. Most young people transition into adulthood. But at only twenty years old, rotating a schedule of days and nights as a new nurse, I was exhausted, and there had been no transition. The positive side to nursing schedules was that I rarely saw my family. Most girls at that time moved in with their family for at least a couple of years after they graduated. But if they did not marry shortly thereafter, they would often get an apartment with a couple of other girls.

Within eight months after I graduated, a ruptured disc became chronically irritated. Even though, at the time, I didn't remember how I had ruptured a disc, lifting heavy patients on hospital nursing floors had finally done me in. I found myself in excruciating pain, hardly able to get out of bed for anything except to use the bathroom. Finally, after five days in bed with muscle spasms causing my back to contort, my mother drove me to an orthopedist who definitively diagnosed a ruptured disc. After another week, I returned to work with pain medications, muscle relaxants, and a tight abdominal corset to keep my back muscles straight. I was alternating heat with ice to relieve the pain from the hard work I was doing for eight hours a day. I lasted another seven months and finally agreed to have my disc removed by a neurosurgeon I knew from my hospital. It was a serious surgery that Mom tried to talk me out of. I'm not sure why she was opposed, but I could not stand living in such pain.

After three months off, I went back to work and felt very confused and wondered where life would lead me since I was still recovering and heavy lifting came with the job. I decided that I would start back to school the next fall to continue my education. I worked part-time to pay my expenses. I could no longer work full-time on an adult medical-surgical unit. I saw a posting for a part-time position to work in the nursery. I had always thought that would be the last place I would want to practice nursing. But I came to love it, especially the neonatal intensive care unit. The babies had such strength and an incredible will to survive. And the nurses in that area were some of the kindest, most fun, and most balanced nurses I had ever worked with. It was a tiring routine of working evenings and going to school during the day. But I loved college classes, and I loved my job. Because I was so frequently gone, I rarely interacted with my parents. I hardly even saw them. I made sure I did all the chores in the house to keep the peace and to prevent any explosions of rage. Otherwise, I pretty much had my own life and found time for friends and dating. Once again, sleep was often sacrificed, but in my youth, I could balance it well. My nursing career would provide me the opportunity to become independent and leave my biological home behind. I would find freedom.

SEEKING FORGIVENESS?

Fast-forward five years from working in the hospital and going to school. Like many of my girlfriends, I had dated, gotten engaged, and married my husband. We had had children and had moved away from my hometown. So much had happened in only five years. I had recovered repressed memories of abuse. I had started to find my way back through the debris from the storm that had left my life in shambles.

It had been weeks since my memories had exploded. On that evening, one of the most important memories I would ever recover was about to give meaning to my entire life. I finally realized why I had survived.

Near the end of a particularly long day, with the kids tucked in bed, I lay on the couch and pulled a throw over my shoulders. I fell into a restless sleep. I awoke with a jolt because the throw was covering my face. It must have shifted up over my neck and shoulders in the restlessness of tossing and turning. I gasped for air. I felt like I was suffocating. That throw blanket over my face was the trigger of a forgotten memory now linked to a strange conversation with my brother Mike when I was a young adult. It was in the 1980s, and we were in the yard of my parents' home. Family members were milling around the cars, talking and finishing conversations before they left for home. It was summer, and the sun was starting to fade. Mike pulled me aside into a conversation of hushed tones. My brother Mike kept saying he was sorry for everything he had done to me in our childhood and needed my forgiveness. He was desperate for me to forgive him. I didn't know what he meant. What was the big deal after all these years, and why was he so insistent about being forgiven?

Was I supposed to forgive all the mean things he used to say and do to me in high school?

Did Mike want instant forgiveness for all the teenage pain and cruelty he had inflicted? He had become more religious and spoke of being saved. I was in my late 20s. I was recently married, was working full time as a nurse, and was building a new home with a new husband.

As I lay in a confused state of semi-wakefulness and felt the throw almost covering my face, I suddenly started to remember a terrible thing that had happened to me. I would soon remember why Mike was pleading for my forgiveness, and it had nothing to do with pot stashes, cruel words, or lies to my parents. As I remembered back, I realized that he thought I remembered what really happened, and suddenly my heart began to beat fast, and that horrible terror took over as the memory started to surface. I tried not to remember. I was exhausted. I tried visualizing a red stop sign in my head and repeating quietly the word "no" over and over, but it was no use. The blurry pieces of that horrible day years earlier were starting to come together. I knew there was no fighting it. I closed my eyes and braced for another memory.

Final Near Death Experience

The memory flooded in with all the force of the other memories that exploded in pictures in my head as if watching the movie unfold and "remembering" what I had long buried. I was about fourteen years old and was being held down on a makeshift table with a long piece of cloth over the hard wood beneath me. There were men surrounding me, and I was making too much noise. Mike was at the head of the table, and he was frantic. He kept telling me to shut up. I continued to protest. He grabbed the closest thing he could. There was an old, white, cotton chenille blanket on the basement floor. He threw it over my face and mouth to muffle my screams. I fought and panicked. My lungs were exploding. No air could move. My head started pounding.

I couldn't scream. I couldn't cry. I was alone. Everything stopped. No panic, no fight, no pain. I never stopped fighting, but Mike thought I did. He didn't realize that I stopped screaming because I stopped breathing. Funny no one even noticed. I stopped screaming from loss of life, not from loss of fight. I was free.

Suddenly I was out of my body and hovering above a group of men. There was complete clarity—no confusion or panic. I sensed that Mike was relieved that he had finally made me shut up. He felt powerful that he had won. Little did he know what trouble he had actually caused. All he knew was that I had stopped screaming and that had been his appointed job.

My father was at the end of the table where the sexual abuse was occurring. I was able to see the makeshift wood table I was lying on and a sheet partially draped over me. My head and torso were covered, but my hand was lying limply. No one knew I wasn't in my body anymore. Why was Mike still pressing down so hard on the blanket? He didn't know I was dead. I thought that odd. My hand was gray, and a light-bluish color formed around the edges of my fingernails.

As I was hovering above the group, I knew what they all were feeling. I heard every thought. My father was self-conscious and afraid he would not be able to have an erection with all the important men there watching. One man was a dentist we knew, and he was thinking how much smarter and better he was than all the other men there. He was the leader. It was very exciting for them to be doing something no one would ever expect of them. After all, they were prominent at their jobs, in the community, and at church. None of the men was thinking anything about me. There was no guilt, no remorse. This was a task that they needed to complete. It was about power and control, not a young girl tied to a table. For them it was not just rape. It was complete control, in complete secrecy, in the middle of the average neighborhood. There was no connection to me as a sister, daughter, and girl. Their thoughts did not overlap, and their feelings did not merge, but I was aware of all thoughts and all feelings separately and yet all at one time. They didn't feel the way normal people did. They were all so empty and void of a normal consciousness. My attention shifted away from the men, and I again noticed my body on the makeshift table balanced on sawhorses, my face covered with the white chenille blanket. Suddenly I was gone from the men and my brother in the dark, musty basement.

I realized I was totally weightless, floating through a long beautiful hallway. Initially I seemed to hover, and then the speed of my ascent propelled me closer and closer toward a brightness that drew me. I had an incredible longing to reach out to that Light. I became aware that everything was different and wonderful. There was no time or space. I was in a place that was completely real and somehow familiar, but it had no boundaries of dimension. As I sped upward, lights so amazingly beautiful pulsed with anticipation. I could not seem to "fly" fast enough. Never had I, nor have I since, wanted anything as desperately as I wanted to reach the Light.

The colors of the lights deepened and glowed in the most incredibly soothing way. They swirled and illuminated a tunnel. As the lights began to magnify the entrance to something incredible, I began to hear, actually sense and feel, music. It was not music as I had ever heard it. It was not the music we know on earth. It was lush and beyond dimension of sound. It was full and focused and was so beautiful, so rich, and so heartfelt that I could barely take it in. The melody was the most harmonious, joyful, angelic, and reverent music I had ever experienced.

The beautiful, vocal, praise, and harp-like melodies arose from beings of glorious reflections of the Light. They were like crystals reflecting the Light, and they hovered and floated around me. The music reached a crescendo that suddenly led to the most intense, reverent stillness as I became engulfed by the sweet, loving, perfect Light.

The Light was not a state of being. The Light was not a consciousness. The Light was a being of love different than any kind of love we experience on earth. I had learned all about God, but this was nothing like I had learned in my religion classes. The Light was the most perfect, complete being of love, knowledge, and acceptance, and I could hardly take it all in. I was entering the meaning of existence, the center of all life and truth and knowing. Although it was the brightest Light I had ever seen, I could look directly into it, and it didn't hurt my eyes. I had only one desire—to stay forever and be enveloped in this Light of perfect love.

I was myself. I was completely and totally the spirit of

me. I was my thoughts, my heart, my individuality, my unique self. I was whole and alive and more myself than I had ever experienced in the confines of my earthly body. I was back to where I began and yet where I had always been. I was complete and whole. The Light was my meaning, my source, the center, the beginning, the end, and the reality of my soul and all that is real. I was home. I was embraced by the Light of the love of God. Surrounding the Light, the vivid colors were beautiful green trees, blue lakes, and animals with intense hues of colors. But there was also something about the images. They were not foggy, shapeless images like we often see in old-fashioned ghost movies. They were clear, crisp spirits with an essence more deep than any real object we see on earth. I did not just see the spirit of the person, but I felt it and smelled and tasted the person's essence. All of the sense experiences we know were so intense. Smells and sounds and sight were all magnified millions of times over. I knew these spirits knew me and loved me as friends and family that had died before me. Their smiles and arms enfolded me. They were truly happy. There was laughter and joy, but not as we know it. It was sweet and robust and deeper joy than you could ever imagine. I was overcome with gratitude and a sense of belonging. No one had ever wanted me or wanted to be with me. But this beautiful, immense Light of God wanted me—truly wanted to hold me like I had never known or have never known since. I have never experienced such love, such joy, such complete acceptance. The Light was proud of me, rejoicing to be with me just because of who I was. As I was enveloped by the Light and perfect love, I became one with all goodness, all kindness, and all perfect harmony, and I knew that this was the source from which all compassion, strength, truth, joy, knowledge, and hope emanated.

While this sounds as if I am recounting a sequence of events, it was not. There was no time; no minutes elapsed. All was instant. There was no past or present. All time was in the exact moment. There were no words spoken, but all was understood. The only way I can try to share this dimensionless realm of no time and no space is to use words, and they are so limiting. There really were angels singing the music—but without notes or voices. These were not angels like we see in pictures. They were real. They surround us.

The Light was holding me with arms of perfect love. I was completely known by the Light. The Light knew my thoughts, my life, my weaknesses, my strengths, my fears, my joys. The Light knew because I was from the Light, created by the Light, always with the Light and so completely and totally loved by the Light. I realized in that instant an awareness that I had forgotten. I had never been alone. In all my childhood, in all my trials, in all my pain, the Light had always been with me. Maybe the overwhelming secrets, pain, terror, and sadness had numbed my spirit, but now I remembered. That is how I had survived all the pain and sadness. I was held up by the Light and by my angel even from infancy. My earthly conscious mind had forgotten this wonderful and comforting truth. I had never been alone.

Never. God had bathed me in love and sent me an angel to comfort me through all of the abuse, for all of my childhood. This *place* of heaven was astonishing and real. This serene dwelling of celebration and worship and joy was merely the reflection of the one who was being praised. I knew. The angels knew. Family and friends who met me knew. The beautiful lights knew. All of creation sang in celebration of the knowledge of the center, the source, the God of all.

I have tried to explain an experience that is beyond description. I have tried to use the limitations of words, time, space, and earthly knowledge to describe the indescribable. How can I use a word like God to describe this incredible essence of love? How can I describe a color no one has ever seen before? How can I share the sweetness of fragrances only heaven knows? How can I explain a place that is not a place at all but is more real than the reality we know on earth? How can I explain spirits that had no dimension but were more complete and true than any human person? How can I explain music that was so beautiful I cannot begin to even explain the first chain of that love melody? Using the word "God" seems disrespectful for such an immense power of love. Using the word "Heaven" seems absurdly simple for the exquisite dwelling place of the Light. The limitation of my ability to describe God and God's dwelling place does not make the perfect love of the Light or heaven any less real. While it was not a place defined in space, it was the reality, the truth, and the love from which we all emanate.

My biggest challenge, however, after knowing heaven and being embraced by the perfect love of God, is not my inability to explain heaven but how to understand earth. God was complete and whole and perfect love. Earth is confusion and limited and while sometimes incredibly wonderful, it can often be very painful. And as I saw the joyous faces of people who had come before me to heaven, saw dogs and animals of all sorts playing in the green grass, watched as angels sang the sweetest love songs and gazed at the beauty of the lakes and trees and flowers—all celebrating and praising God, I suddenly became aware of a choice I had to make. Stay or return. It was my choice. I knew what would happen if I did return, as the horror of what I was returning to had not changed. I knew God's plans. Still melting into the loving arms of God, I was conscious of the abuse. How could such evil cruelty happen in the presence of the Light? That question had an instant response. Suddenly the love, peace, and joy of the Light turned into the most intense, profound sadness. The pain of that sorrow was more than I could bear. The same Light that loves us so immensely allows us the ability to choose our actions as humans. If God intervened in every act of violence, every act of hatred, every act of cruelty, then there would be no free will. But I became aware of the pain God's heart suffers when we pull away from his perfect love and hurt others. That helps define sin. We literally break God's heart when we choose not to grow, love, or use our gifts. God abhors evil. Evil is darkness, the opposite of God's Light. Yet I became completely aware of the enormity of the love of the Light. Evil cannot exist except as a creation of the Light that has chosen darkness. And that can only happen when a person chooses that darkness. In that same moment, I saw an image revealed to me. There was a massive, unending ocean. One drop fell in that ocean. God revealed to me the depth and breadth of his love was like that ocean, and evil was just a drop in the ocean of the love of God.

If we couldn't choose, then we couldn't choose to love rather than hate. We couldn't choose to forgive rather than become bitter or retaliate. We would not be able to create and share God's love on earth if He did not give us the opportunity to choose to do so. That was the answer to how God could allow me to be so abused. Free will. But God's gift of free will and our ability to choose how we treat others and how we turn our back on God comes with a price. Our choice to turn away from God's love, no matter how slight or how intensely evil, creates a separation from God's perfect love and breaks the heart of God. Literally. Instantly, the intensity of that sadness turned into the most compassionate love I have ever known. I knew that no matter what happened to me if I went back, no matter how lonely I felt, or how scared I would be, or how hurt I was, I would never be alone. My spirit would always be loved, held, and covered by the Light of God and the gift of a comforting angel to pull me away from the pain as it occurred. While that may sound simple, it was enormously comforting. I had never been and would never be alone.

The instant I chose to return to my human life, I slammed back into my body. I was back in the basement. The dentist was cussing, my arm burned, and my heart was beating so hard I thought it might explode out of my chest. I felt unsteady and foggy, but through the blur of activity, I saw a syringe and needle. I didn't know what had happened, but everyone was standing around my half-naked body. There was a palpable mixture of terror and relief. I heard the dentist swearing. Angry that I had died, the dentist shouted that if he hadn't brought me back, how did they think they were going to cover it up? He swore at them and told them how stupid they all were. Mike untied my arms and legs. My father threw my school uniform and white shirt at me. I was embarrassed getting dressed in front of them, but I didn't need to be. No one cared about me, Jane. I was just a liability. Soon everyone scurried out of the basement. I was the last up the stairs, and I went straight to my room. Holly was barking at the window, and everything was still a blur. I wanted out of my clothes and went in to take a shower. I had a dull, throbbing headache, and the anxiety made my hands shake. I wasn't sure if it had just been a long day at school or if I was worried about a test the next day. The warm water washed over me, calming me as I took slow deep breaths.

NO ONE CAN TOUCH YOUR SPIRIT

I sat up on the couch; the throw that had slipped over my head was now around my shoulders. The kids had gone to bed. I grabbed my journal and began to write. I wrote of the strange interaction with Mike when I was in my twenties. I finally realized exactly what had happened and why he had begged for forgiveness. And I wrote of the Light. The beautiful, perfect, love of the Light. I also wrote many questions. As I write this story now, I still have the same thoughts and questions. That day in the basement was depraved abuse, but the experience paled in comparison to my presence in the Light. How could I possibly have survived abuse that was so horrible that I died? How could I be emotionally stable and loving and trusting? That night journaling, I realized that my final near-death experience was profound. All these years later, I have come to understand the depth of the impact it had on my life. My spirit came out of my body and then returned. The body is what I use to exist in the world. My true self, my essence, floated above that body, went to the Light, and returned to that body.

No matter what happens to our body, nothing can ever touch our spirits. No matter what my family did to my body, no matter what they physically forced me to do, no matter how cruel, how brutal, or how inhumane, nothing could touch my spirit. My essence is completely a reflection of God's love. No hate, no abuse, no cruelty could ever dim that Light of God in my soul. We all emanate from that perfect Light of God, and nothing that happens to us can tarnish our spirits. Nothing. You and I and all of creation have one source, and that is the Light of God. That gives me hope. It helps me connect with others. It helps me see love. It helps me accept love. We truly are of the same fiber, the same love, the same essence. We all were created in the radiant, perfect love of the Light of God. Before I put down the journal for the evening, I made one last entry. I actually wrote a simple prayer, a prayer of gratitude. "Thank you, God." Thank God I died. I have repeated that prayer every day of my life since that memory. Thank God I died.

The Whisper of God

My spirit, my true essence, chose to come back to the confines of my body and to the earthly realm. I came back changed. While I would not remember until decades later, I had seen the face of God and was enveloped by the love of the Light. My being, my spirit, my consciousness, and my heart had been opened to the reason we are here on earth. We are here to love. We are here to create loving relationships. We are here to stretch beyond our fears and bridge the chasm of linear thinking and reach out to the limitless love of God. That metamorphosis is difficult, painful, continuous, and challenging. We cannot do that alone. It is impossible. Only the love of the Light has the power and gentleness to change our hearts. Most exist in their ego-based mentality. To change—love and accept love, forgive and accept forgiveness, grieve, grow, and stretch beyond our three-dimensional existence—we must learn how to do what humans rarely do. Be silent. Be still. Accept.

Only in silence will we hear the whisper of God. Only in stillness can we truly experience the timeless dimension of the love of the Light. We must accept the moment we are in. There is no time within the Light. We exist in a world of limitations, of dimension, of time constraints, of ego, of impatience, of pain and suffering, and of joy, delight, confusion, chaos, and even evil, and therein lies the challenge. If we focus on the pain, suffering, chaos and all other earthly constraints, then we separate ourselves from God. It is painfully simple. First acknowledge the separation. Then be silent. Silence takes commitment, practice, and patience. Be still. We want instant answers, formulaic solutions, and we want to bargain. That is not what God desires. God wants you to be still. Sit in stillness and allow pure silence to overtake you; then you are entering into the presence of God. Accept the moment—that pure, timeless, perfect moment—and the Light will embrace you. As you move through your days and nights, you will hear the gentle whisper of God. There is a constant struggle between your ego wanting control and allowing God to be your wise and gentle guide. That is the ongoing struggle. We cannot change the world. We sadly cannot stop all child abuse. We cannot fight evil. But God can. Be still. Listen to the silence. Practice acceptance. Allow the love of the Light to embrace you. You will hear whispers. Then you will be led.

I chose to come back to my body. I chose to come back to this earthly existence with a clear purpose. There are times when I realize, "I know I knew this in the Light." That knowing happened at the births of my children. It happens when I pick up the phone to call someone, already knowing that something is very wrong before that person even tells me. It has happened when I have helped patients as they naturally left this earth and watched as their spirits exited their bodies.

I could have stayed. Oh how I wanted to remain embraced by the Light of God. But I knew I had to come back. My beautiful children would not have been born. This book of truth and hope would not have been written. The relationship with my husband, my friendships, the joy of the dogs in my life, the laughter I share—none of those important moments would ever have been realized.

Life has not been charmed and easy. There have been plenty of times I questioned why I came back to this place of pain and frustration. Yes, there is love. Yes, there is joy. But there is also pain, hurt, confusion, and exhaustion. But that is exactly when I have to be silent and still and accept. The world pulls so hard at us to act, to move, to decide, to jump. But we must remember that God calls us to be still. In that stillness, God may guide us to take action. Doors will open to a counselor, a book, a friendship, or a significant self-awareness, and in those experiences God calls us to grow, to stretch, and to lean into our fear and pain. Be silent and be still, and when you hear the whisper of God, accept.

There is another lesson I learned in the Light. After I recovered my memories, I went through every stage of grieving many times over. I have seen some survivors of abuse get stuck in the stages of grieving, but that only keeps you from healing. As hard as it was, maybe because I had been to the Light and in the presence of the love of God, I knew I had to forgive. I couldn't do it myself. But I could consciously choose to ask God to forgive my abusers through me. That took enormous strength, and I did it. That was the beginning of the greatest healing that I have experienced.

Forgiveness allowed me to move forward knowing that I did not have to judge. I knew that there was probably generational abuse, mental illness, and most likely evil in those who hurt me. But I did not have to sort all that out. Sadly, the members of my family of origin proved they were dangerous. I was in self-preservation mode, but more than that, I was absolutely committed to shielding my children from that family. Even though I never saw evidence of sorrow or even ownership of their actions, I could still forgive. I did this for me. I did this so I could move on. I did this so I could love and share in love with my family and friends. I did not need to stay in the past. I grieved, I mourned, and I accepted. I will never understand why that was my childhood. I chose to become better and not bitter. Forgiveness does not forget. No, even after forgiveness, the memories stay intact to teach you. But what forgiveness does do is take away the need to blame and seek revenge, which will ravage you from the inside out. God has it all covered. Here's a simple action with profound implication: Ask God to forgive through you so you can move on with your life in love.

I Told the Truth

The statistics are pretty bleak with respect to remaining in a marriage after memories of abuse have surfaced. We had gone to counseling on and off for most of our marriage before and after the memories. I was a completely different person than the person who said the vows in her early twenties. We had almost separated the year after my memories surfaced, but we hadn't. Family is so incredibly important to me, and I couldn't risk not being in my children's lives.

When we did not separate initially, a part of me went into a type of hibernation. I found a new survival mode. I became Mom, and our lives revolved around the kids. I had to be hypervigilant, keeping them safe from my biological family. At the same time, they needed to grow, laugh, and enjoy childhood like I had never been able to do. I would stay aware and alert but would never project that fear onto them.

Remember the threats I heard from Anthony and my father? Remember what they said would happen if I ever told what happened to me? It made absolutely no sense to me as a child. How could they threaten to find me when I grew up and do the same thing to my kids and kill us all? It made no sense as a child. I was the child. But those threats were embedded in my memory. Now as an adult, I felt the full impact of those childhood threats. Repeating them to me so often was an intimidation technique to terrorize me so much that I would never speak of my abuse.

That is why I was terrified when I spoke of my abuse at thirty-two years old. I told! My husband called my father. My husband's exact words are seared in my memory. He told my father, "Jane remembers everything of her childhood. Don't call or try to contact us, or we will call the police." He never even used the word "abuse." My father's responded, "I can't believe I'm hearing this." That was all he said. Those strange six words were all he said. If my son-in-law called me out of the blue one day and told me that my daughter remembered everything of her childhood and not to contact them, my response would be much different. It would make no sense to me at all. With a few expletives, I would respond with "What the 'bleep' are you talking about? Remembers what? Is she OK? Let me talk to her now! *I'm* calling the police!" And I would. I would also jump in a car or on a plane and immediately go to my daughter's home. I'd be terrified for her safety and her children's safety. Again, compare that to my father's response: "I can't believe I'm hearing this."

My father-in-law was retired military. He relied on facts. My abuse was difficult for him to process. My father's response convinced him that my abuse was true because, he said, "No innocent father would respond the way your dad did. And for that matter, I would welcome the police!"

We took no chances. We changed our phone number, forwarded all mail to a PO Box to intercept any threatening mail, and moved from the home where they knew we lived. We got a top-notch security system, and we legally changed our name.

Abuse is hard to prove, especially decades later. We spoke with a district attorney in the county where we were living. We also spoke to an attorney who specialized in representing clients in cases similar to mine involving the recovery of repressed memories. They told us the truth. It would be difficult, if not impossible, to prove, and it would only prolong the healing process I had started. I had no desire for retribution. I just wanted my own family to be safe. There was no substantial physical evidence of the abuse, so I couldn't even get restraining orders. The one thing that was at the heart of all the abuse was secrecy. That was their power, and that led to the constant programming threats of future harm if I ever told what happened. So Jill told me my greatest protection was the truth. My husband sent a certified letter to the abusers. It was clear and direct. If there was any attempt to contact me, or my husband and kids, or if any harm or harassment came upon any of us, we would go directly to the media. We promised to use every means possible to name the abusers and explicitly detail the abuse. Their greatest fear was being exposed and humiliated. Truth was *my* power.

Did anyone from my extended family try to contact us? No. No one in my family reached out. Not then, not ever. No representative or lawyer called on their behalf. There were no unexpected knocks at the door or letters in the mail to try to establish contact. Bizarre, unless they were guilty and scared of the truth damaging their reputation and bringing shame upon them.

I once thought a man was following me during a day of errands in the city with the kids. His car seemed to be at several of my stops. Was he a private investigator, or was it just a coincidence? I never knew, and it never happened again. I was pretty vigilant for those first few years. Just when I started to let my guard down, an alarming incident happened at my youngest child's bus stop. It just so happened that my youngest was sick on the day that a car pulled up to a school bus stop and blocked the bus from moving. The bus driver and kids described two older adults in the car. The bus driver had to park and get out of the bus to ask them to move. She didn't recognize the name of the child they were asking about because my child had a nickname my parents would never have known since communication had been cut off for years. My husband's parents were on a trip to China, so we knew it could not be them. Unfortunately, no license plate number was obtained, but a records search showed that the type of car that stopped the bus matched the type of car my parents owned. I was terrified. I found my parents' phone number on the Internet. We had a police officer call them and warn them to stay away and tell them we didn't want anything to do with them. My father stated he had no idea what the officer was talking about. He denied being in our town until the police officer gave him the exact description of the car that matched his. He became silent when she warned they would be on the lookout for his car in the area. It was, and still is, terrifying to think of what my parents wanted and what they planned to do. While my children always knew that I had been abused, I had deliberately refused to share the depth of my terror surrounding this incident. But my hypervigilance was on high alert once again. Do I still look over my shoulder? Sometimes. The degree of fear and even terror has diminished over the years, but I have never minimized the horror of the abuse they inflicted. I came to forgive, but I will never, ever forget.

Even After the Light, I Am Still Very Human

As my children grew older, stronger, and more independent, I went to work full-time when my husband was looking for a job. I was not a nurse in a hospital this time, but in a technical area of health care called informatics. The pay was extremely good. I saw I had skills and strengths besides nursing. I was supporting our family, and it changed me. I was no longer financially dependent on my husband—as I had grown to believe I was. New friends, teamwork, and professional environments created a more confident me. I realized that many of the sound bites of our marriage and self-held beliefs were false. I was capable of supporting our family. I was a good mom and a good provider. These changes and realizations exacerbated the cracks in our marriage. It became painfully evident that I was very, very tired. I made the most painful and difficult decision of my life and left the marriage. Wow! Talk about alone! No family of origin. A single mom. I was terrified and relieved at the same time. I needed to heal and grow. Our divorce was hard on my kids. It broke my heart to see them suffer through it. The pain of the divorce felt like it outweighed that of my childhood abuse. This pain resulted from a decision I made, not from what others chose to do to me. I knew, however, that to survive I had to leave. My emotional and physical health depended on a new start for us all. We all needed to heal, and relationships needed to mend. After almost five years of time to reflect, grow, and receive more counseling, I met a wonderfully supportive, intelligent, funny, and kind man. We have been married for several wonderful years. I had dated, but I never became serious until I met Rob. I had never known peace my entire life. So slowly and gently, Rob and I paved a path, one stone at a time, creating a new and loving marriage. Joining the two families and trying to find our places with each of the kids was at times exciting and fun and at other times painful. We have all grown. My children are young adults, marrying and creating their own paths. My children have always known about my abuse but probably could never really reconcile the enormity of what happened to me. I was their mom. That is all they ever knew. My abuse never interfered with picnics on the family room floor with a vinyl tablecloth, raising puppies, learning to read, bedtime stories, medicine for ear infections, quiet time, learning that words hurt, sharing Christmases and birthdays, doing chores every week (yes, really, every week), walks to the park, or shuttles throughout the city to sports or school-related activities. I was just Mom. I was always there. And while they acknowledged that my abuse was bad, I don't think it was ever much of a factor relating to their lives, but more just something that happened to me when I was young.

They did not realize, however, that I had absolutely no role model or help to raise them. I did everything opposite of what was done to me, and I prayed for guidance. I prayed a lot! I never abused them. My youngest even got mad once and yelled, "Why do you stay so calm? Why can't you just scream at me like other moms?" We laugh about that now, but I grew up with a mother who screamed and followed that with devastating silent treatment. Even as she stood in the same room and sat at the same table, I was invisible. I knew the damage and pain she could inflict. Counseling has taught me a lot. When I get angry, I find my voice usually gets very quiet. I refuse to erupt. We discuss our feelings. I have learned a lot and stopped a lot of cycles. But as I have told my kids, I am not perfect. I goof up as a friend, a wife, a mom, a human being. I may have been to the Light, but I am back in this very real life and am very human. Having had a near-death experience as intense as mine does not make me a saint. Far from it. I still get up every morning and go to work. I still get frustrated with people, and people get frustrated with me. I get irritated if someone cuts me off in traffic and nearly causes an accident. I laugh and play jokes and have a good sense of humor. And I cry. My feelings get hurt. Just because I saw God's bigger picture, I still have to live in my smaller one. I get scared when my kids are sick. I still have my scars from childhood and hear my mom calling me a spoiled brat when I ask for something I need. I am human. My imperfect, human self tries to take one moment at a time. I am still on this journey of life and learning. But I have a gift. I know the Light. I often reflect on this quote from St. Francis of Assisi: "All the darkness in the world cannot extinguish the light of a single candle."

We will all struggle, and we are all pulled by our ego and life and exhaustion and time and deadlines and frustrations and joys and triumphs. That will all pass. It is good. We are all loved. You are loved.

STOPPING THE CYCLE

No one can hide, and I knew I couldn't either. With the advent of social media, it has become easy to peek at the family I left behind. But on one particular day recently, something caused me to pull out this laptop and get this book done. On a social media site, I saw one of my sisters. She was alive and well in a picture in front of the Sleeping Beauty Castle at Disneyland in a Disney shirt and smiling from ear to ear next to her husband. That was it! They were all living their lives as if nothing ever happened! I learned from a hometown friend that this smiling sister was the same sister who was collecting disability because she was physically unable to work due to a stress-related disorder. She was suddenly afflicted after I spoke the truth of my memories. But there she was, smiling for the camera for the entire world to see. That was the push I needed.

I had literally survived death, and there they were, standing in front of Disneyland as if nothing had happened! That smile, the facade, the pretending. That is the whole point—this is not pretend. Child abuse is real! I suffered horribly and am still worn out with frustration on days when I read about yet another teacher or respected family member who abused a child. We can't live in a make-believe world and smile for the camera when we know the truth. I have shared only a few stories of my abuse. There were so, so many more. If my words stop one person from being abused because I raised awareness and the abuse was reported, then it will have been worth my effort. If one person gets help for his or her own abuse because of my story, then all the writing will have been worth it. Then we can really go to a theme park and celebrate with authentic smiles. Let's stop the cycle of abuse. Let's all work together to be more aware. Let's pray that our children stay safe, but let's not live in a fantasy world where we ignore the signs. Together we can stop the cycle from perpetuating itself, generation after generation, and we can allow children to experience their childhood in a safe and healthy world.

What To Do If You Suspect a Child Is Being Abused

I am convinced that teachers, other parents, doctors, and extended family saw clear signs of my abuse but chose not to act. I want you to act. I want you to be aware. Watch for signs of abuse. One in four children are abused before the age of eighteen. The results can be devastating.

If you have a gut feeling that a child is struggling, trust it. Tell someone. Ask advice from a counselor. Call the police. You can report anonymously and set up a case file, which helps enormously in the event another report is made on that same child. Be available to a child. Just be a friend. If the child wants to open up to you, he or she will. If not, don't push. Your kindness alone may change a life forever. And please remember to balance common sense with awareness.

We have learned that hysteria helps no one. Trust your gut, and get some advice from professionals who know how to address potential abuse.

Silence is the enemy. Silence perpetuates abuse. Silence allows victims to become abusers and allows the cycle to continue generation after generation.

If you have been abused and never told anyone, make an appointment with a trained counselor. Call someone you trust. Talk about it. Bring it out into the light and surround yourself with friends and healthy family members. Get professional help. You can heal. There is hope!

Let's all move forward together to protect our children. Thank you for reading a bit of my story. We can change the world one child at a time.

HELPFUL INFORMATION

Child Abuse Signs and Symptoms (Mayoclinic.org)

Behavioral
- Withdrawal from friends or usual activities
- Changes in behavior—such as aggression, anger, hostility, or hyperactivity—or changes in school performance
- Depression, anxiety, unusual fears, or a sudden loss of self-confidence
- An apparent lack of supervision
- Frequent absences from school or reluctance to ride the school bus
- Reluctance to leave school activities, as if he or she

doesn't want to go home
- Attempts at running away
- Rebellious or defiant behavior
- Attempts at suicide

Specific signs and symptoms depend on the type of abuse and can vary. Keep in mind that warning signs are just that—warning signs. The presence of warning signs doesn't necessarily mean that a child is being abused.

Physical abuse signs and symptoms
- Unexplained injuries, such as bruises, fractures, or burns
- Injuries that don't match the given explanation
- Untreated medical or dental problems

Sexual abuse signs and symptoms
- Sexual behavior or knowledge that's inappropriate for the child's age
- Pregnancy or a sexually transmitted infection
- Blood in the child's underwear
- Statements that he or she was sexually abused
- Trouble walking or sitting or complaints of genital pain
- Abuse of other children sexually

Emotional abuse signs and symptoms
- Delayed or inappropriate emotional development
- Loss of self-confidence or self-esteem
- Social withdrawal or a loss of interest or enthusiasm
- Depression
- Headaches or stomachaches with no medical cause
- Avoidance of certain situations, such as refusing to go to school or ride the bus
- Desperate seeking of affection
- A decrease in school performance or loss of interest in school
- Loss of previously acquired developmental skills

Neglect signs and symptoms
- Poor growth or weight gain
- Poor hygiene
- Lack of clothing or supplies to meet physical needs
- Taking food or money without permission
- Eating a lot in one sitting or hiding food for later
- Poor record of school attendance
- Lack of appropriate attention for medical, dental, or psychological problems or lack of necessary follow-up care
- Emotional swings that are inappropriate or out of context for the situation
- Indifference

Child Abuse and Neglect Consequences (CDC.gov)

Prevalence: One in Four Children Suffer Abuse
- An estimated 702,000 children were confirmed by child protective services as being victims of abuse and neglect in 2014.
- At least one in four children have experienced child neglect or abuse (including physical, emotional, and sexual) at some point in their lives, and one in seven children experienced abuse or neglect in the last year.

Effects: Child Abuse and Neglect Affect Children Now and Later
- Improper brain development
- Impaired cognitive (learning ability) and socio-emotional (social and emotional) skills
- Lower language development
- Blindness, cerebral palsy from head trauma
- Higher risk for heart, lung, and liver diseases, obesity, cancer, high blood pressure, and high cholesterol
- Anxiety
- Smoking, alcoholism, and drug abuse

Physical
- In 2014, approximately 1,580 children died from abuse and neglect across the country—a rate of 2.13 deaths per 100,000 children.

- Abuse and neglect during infancy or early childhood can cause regions of the brain to form and function improperly with long-term consequences on cognitive and language abilities, socio-emotional development, and mental health.[3] For example, the stress of chronic abuse may cause a "hyperarousal" response in certain areas of the brain, which may result in hyperactivity and sleep disturbances.
- Children may experience severe or fatal head trauma as a result of abuse. Nonfatal consequences of abusive head trauma include varying degrees of visual impairment (e.g., blindness), motor impairment (e.g., cerebral palsy) and cognitive impairments.
- Children who experience abuse and neglect are also at increased risk for adverse health effects and certain chronic diseases as adults, including heart disease, cancer, chronic lung disease, liver disease, obesity, high blood pressure, high cholesterol, and high levels of C-reactive protein.

Psychological
- In one long-term study, as many as 80 percent of young adults who had been abused met the diagnostic criteria for at least one psychiatric disorder at age twenty-one. These young adults exhibited many problems, including depression, anxiety, eating disorders, and suicide attempts.

- The stress of chronic abuse may result in anxiety and may make victims more vulnerable to problems such as post-traumatic stress disorder, conduct disorder, and learning, attention, and memory difficulties.

Behavioral
- Children who experience abuse and neglect are at increased risk for smoking, alcoholism, and drug abuse as adults, as well as engaging in high-risk sexual behaviors.
- Those with a history of child abuse and neglect are 1.5 times more likely to use illicit drugs, especially marijuana, in middle adulthood.
- Studies have found abused and neglected children to be at least 25 percent more likely to experience problems such as delinquency, teen pregnancy, and low academic achievement.[13] Similarly, a longitudinal study found that physically abused children were at greater risk of being arrested as juveniles, being a teen parent, and being less likely to graduate from high school.
- A National Institute of Justice study indicated that being abused or neglected as a child increased the likelihood of arrest as a juvenile by 59 percent. Abuse and neglect also increased the likelihood of adult criminal behavior by 28 percent and violent crime by 30 percent.

- Child abuse and neglect can have a negative effect on the ability of both men and women to establish and maintain healthy intimate relationships in adulthood.

Economic
- The total lifetime economic burden resulting from new cases of fatal and nonfatal child abuse and neglect in the United States in 2008 was approximately $124 billion in 2010 dollars. This economic burden rivaled the cost of other high-profile public health problems, such as stroke and Type 2 diabetes.
- The estimated average lifetime cost per victim of nonfatal child abuse and neglect was $210,012 (in 2010 dollars), including the following:
- Childhood health care costs
- Adult medical costs
- Productivity losses
- Child welfare costs
- Criminal justice costs
- Special education costs

REFERENCES

Centers for Disease Control and Prevention. (2016, April 05). Child Abuse and Neglect: Consequences. Retrieved from https://www.cdc.gov/ViolencePrevention/childmaltreatment/consequences.html

Colman, R. A., & Widom, C. S. (2004). Childhood abuse and neglect and adult intimate relationships: A prospective study. *Child Abuse & Neglect, 28*(11), 1133-1151.

Danese, A., Moffitt, T. E., Harrington, H., Milne, B. J., Polanczyk, G., Pariante, C. M., ... Caspi, A. (2009). Adverse Childhood Experiences and Adult Risk Factors for Age-Related Disease: Depression, Inflammation, and Clustering of Metabolic Risk Markers. *Archives of Pediatrics & Adolescent Medicine, 163*(12), 1135–1143.

Fang, X, Brown, D. S., Florence, C. S. & Mercy, J. A. (2012). The economic burden of child maltreatment in the United States and implications for prevention. *Child Abuse & Neglect, 36*(2), 156-165.

Farley, R. H., M.S., Loveless, B., Palusci, V. J., M.D., & Taroli, A., M.D. (2014). *Recognizing When a Child's Injury or Illness Is Caused by Abuse* (U.S. Department of Justice, Office of Juvenile Justice and Delinquency Prevention). Washington, D.C. Retrieved from https://www.ojjdp.gov/pubs/243908.pdf

Fitzgibbons, R., Dr. (2004, May 1). Seminary Reform Needed in Wake of Sex Abuse Study [Interview by ZENIT]. Retrieved from https://www.ewtn.com/library/ISSUES/ZSEMREFO.HTM

Gilbert, L. K., M.D., Breiding, M. J., PhD, Merrick, M. T., PhD, Thompson, W. W., PhD, Ford, D. C., PhD, Dhingra, S. S., MPH, & Parks, S. E., PhD. (2015). Childhood Adversity and Adult Chronic Disease. *American Journal of Preventative Medicine, 48*(3), 345-349.

Heisler, K., PhD. (2014). *Child Maltreatment*(U.S. Department of Health & Human Services, Administration for Children and Families, Administration on Children, Youth, and Families, Children's Bureau). Retrieved from http://www.acf.hhs.gov/sites/default/files/cb/cm2014.pdf

Hopper, J., PhD. Unwanted or Abusive Childhood Experiences. Retrieved February 01, 2017 from https://www.jimhopper.com/child-abuse/overview/

Kirk, M., & Boyer, P. J. (Writers). (2002, April 25). Did Daddy Do It? [Television series episode]. In *Frontline*. PBS.

Mayo Clinic Staff. (2015, October 07). Child abuse: Coping, support and prevention. Retrieved February 1, 2017 from http://www.mayoclinic.org/diseases-conditions/child-abuse/basics/symptoms/con-20033789

Nakazawa, D. J. (2015). *Childhood disrupted: how your biography becomes your biology, and how you can heal*. New York: Atria Paperback.

National Alliance on Mental Illness. Dissociative Disorders. Retrieved February 01, 2017 from http://www.nami.org/Learn-More/Mental-Health-Conditions/Dissociative-Disorders

Perry, B. (2009). How we remember. *Child and Youth Care Network-Online*, (122). Retrieved from http://www.cyc-net.org/cyc-online/cyconline-apr2009-perry.html

Silverman, A. B., Reinherz, H. Z., & Giaconia, R. M. (1996). The long-term sequelae of child and adolescent abuse: A longitudinal community study. *Child Abuse & Neglect, 20*(8), 709-723.

Widom, C. S., Marmorstein, N. R., & Raskin White, H. (2006). Childhood victimization and illicit drug use in middle adulthood. Psychology of Addictive Behaviors, 20(4), 394-403.

Widom, C. S., & Maxfield, M. G. (2001). *An Update on the "Cycle of Violence"*(U.S. Department of Justice, Office of Justice Programs). Washington, D.C.: National Institute of Justice. Retrieved from: http://www.ncjrs.gov/pdffiles1/nij/184894.pdf

Important Phone Numbers

If you or someone you know needs help,
please call one of the following numbers:

National Association of Adult Survivors of Child Abuse:
323-552-6150

National Child Abuse Hotline: Hotline:
1-800-4ACHILD

National Suicide Prevention Lifeline:
1-800-273-8255

www.ingramcontent.com/pod-product-compliance
Lightning Source LLC
Chambersburg PA
CBHW031443040426
42444CB00007B/948